GASLIGHTING
ABUSE RECOVERY
FOR WOMEN

Gaslighting Abuse Recovery for Women

Self Help Guide to Heal From Psychological Abuse and Survive Narcissistic Manipulation, How to Rebuild Healthy Relationships and Improve Your Self Esteem

JESSICA ELLEN HAMMOCK

Copyright

Contents

Introduction

Introduction

Congratulations on your purchase of *Gaslighting Abuse Recovery for Women*, and thank you for doing so. This book provides information about the insidious domestic violence of gaslighting. By purchasing this book, you show any interest in learning more about the subject. You may even know someone victimized.

Any form of abuse can be hard to understand. Gaslighting is no exception. Generally, it can be subtle and covert, making gaslighting more treacherous than physical abuse since gaslighting hits a person's mental faculties and tugs on emotional strings. For any person to surrender their perception of reality for someone else's opinions, something extreme must have occurred. Whenever a person loses their beliefs, thoughts, hope, and ideas, the world turns dangerous for that individual. The peril is similar to a reckless hypnotist putting you under, convincing you that you are a chicken, and telling you to cross the road.

Before going any further, let me preface this by saying that each person carries the responsibility for their actions. An individual should never allow anyone to convince you otherwise! The victims of another person's actions hold no responsibility for those actions.

Inside of this book, you will find no one belittling you or tearing you down. However, you will discover that this aggressive, offensive, and abusive treatment is widespread and not limited to one individual. We will provide you with an understanding that will help you make significant changes in your life.

Domestic violence occurs everywhere in the civilized world with no exemptions. The signs of physical abuse speak for themselves. However, psychological and emotional abuse often eludes detection until the victim receives severe damage. The 2019 statistics in the US for psychological abuse show that over 48% of the respondents suffered at least one incident of psychological aggression by an intimate partner. That is nearly half of the represented population in a cross-population study, and this fact staggers the mind.

The vows we say when getting married state "love, honor, and obey." However, when one hears of domestic violence, automatic questions should surface. Questions such as "how can hitting demonstrate love or honor?" or "how can coercion show honor?" or "is submission to coercion the same as obey?" To all these questions, I now respond with a firm "NO."

Years ago, a husband moved his wife, four young children, and their pets to a lovely house on half of an acre of land. The family consisted of a 9-year-old daughter, a 4-year-old son, a 2-year-old daughter, a 3-month-old son, a hamster, and a mama cat with two kittens. The house had indoor plumbing and electricity but no phone service. The property was 10 miles from town, and the closest neighbor was two miles away.

At the time, the husband was a truck driver, and he would be gone for six weeks at a time. When he came home from a road trip, he would only be there for five days. Every time he went out, he would remove the distributor cap from his wife's car with the coil and rotor. He held her and the children in captive isolation in that house during the weeks he drove over the road.

When the husband was at home, the wife worked up the courage to ask him why he would leave her stranded like that. "It is just a rotor and coil. You should always carry extras." He laughed as he walked away from her. He had made her feel stupid, and melancholy washed over her. Tears began to slip down her face.

Her family was in a different state. And whenever she tried to make a friend or an acquaintance through a school or church function, her husband would run them off. So, she had no one to talk to or turn to when she needed help while he drove. Even though she tried to keep herself confident and busy, these long periods alone wore her down. And she started to believe him that she was useless, stupid, and deserving of his punishments.

Our survivor knows from experience the toll that gaslighting extracts from a person. However, she lived in those intolerable conditions for a long time before suffering a nervous breakdown. Nowadays, she knows better. She considers herself a survivor and prays that more women get away from their abusers. She does not want anyone suffering from gaslighting.

The above illustrates one type of control that people often use – isolation from family and friends. Human beings by nature desire socialization, and over time, its deprivation can lead to mental health issues. Solitary confinement got used for centuries in prisons as a means for controlling inmates. And in prisoner of war camps to break the morale of the prisoners.

During the 1950s through the year 2000, five major

religious cults have used brainwashing and gaslighting tactics on their congregation. Also, in the 1960s and 1970s, three of the most notorious killers used gaslighting techniques on their victims. When gaslighting gets used as a weapon for murder, people need to know how this manipulation method can be fatal. The severe nature of this form of abuse can get described as raping a person's will.

Another opportunity for witnessing the gaslight tactic occurs during elections. Often reports abound about election campaigns leaking disinformation about opponents gets cast around to gaslight the voters. The prevalence of gaslighting throughout history contributes to the staggering statistics of its use and acceptance today to control and coerce people. But the long-term aftereffects can be debilitating to the victims and sometimes fatal.

In this book, we will examine gaslighting from the definition of the term through to the long-term adverse effects. We will uncover some of the history surrounding the term and cover different results that occur. We will diagram the types of people that use gaslighting and signs of being gaslit. While almost anyone can gaslight someone, some specific traits can identify a gaslighter. The crises of identity that ensue from the subjugation can be as profound as a blackened eye. In the final chapters, we will discuss recovering our sense of self-worth and beginning to live our life the way we should. Any form of recovery is always an uphill journey. Still, there is no journey more satisfying than the recovery of oneself.

We know the perceptions of isolation, fear, and confusion that a person going through this form of abuse feels. And how the loneliness closes in on you, devouring all your hope. We understand the need for sucking in your gut, blowing out all the wind, and throwing your shoulders back in a show of false bravado. Only to have my tongue fumbling with blustering words getting rebuked with insults and lies. Then as the smile fades from the lips, the shoulders drop, and tears well up in the eyes, we crawl back into ourselves and wonder how we ever got into this situation.

Please, know that when we say that you are not alone. Some individuals do not understand how to love anyone else or do not know how to express themselves. And you did not create or request the abuse happening. If you need some hope, be reassured that a better life is waiting outside the prison cell of mental, emotional, and psychological abuse. You will find the ability to cast aside the prison shackles and walk away from the prison warden.

You are a strong individual and survivor with a compassionate heart. If you were not such a person, this bully never would have attempted to enslave you.

Abusers and addicts seek out individuals that will temporarily satisfy unspoken and indistinct needs. If they perceive you as intimidating, you present a challenge to them. If they think of you as a helpless child, they will rush to the rescue to protect you from the outside world; little do they know that you need protection from them.

In chapter one, we discuss the term gaslighting, what it means and how the term originated. Trauma gets discussed since extreme stress can traumatize a person. The term narcissism gets introduced since many professionals link narcissism with gaslighting. You can find different examples of gaslighting throughout the book to assist with explanations.

Hints and clues found in chapter two can help a person decide if they are a victim of gaslighting. Some of the known techniques provide an insight into how someone accomplishes gaslighting. Some commonly spoken phrases are listed to assist with identifying gaslighting. Gaslighting may be covert, but if you know what to pay attention to, gaslighting becomes easier to detect.

The most common personality types that employ gaslighting get presented in chapter three. The characteristics and behaviors of these personality types can help a person identify who resides with them. Typical attributes to the kind of person that seems to fall prey to gaslighters are listed. And half a dozen phrases are provided that can stop a gaslighting attempt.

Chapter four offers an in-depth summary of gaslighting techniques and stages, along with examples. Common phrases are listed to assist in identifying possible gaslighting exposure. Merely calling someone crazy once does not mean anyone gets gaslit. However, if several actions from chapter four occur along with being called crazy, the person would benefit from reflection on the guidance, scenes, and experience found on these pages.

Chapter five discusses the different mental and emotional states that a gaslit person might develop over time. And the seriousness of these conditions. Further trauma will present signs and symptoms since prolonged exposure to abuse inevitably leads to some trauma.

Chapter six reviews ways of recovering with and without therapies. Different forms of treatment receive discussion and practices for the gaslighting survivor to rejoin society. There are self-help techniques provided but by no means are these substitutes for counseling. Victims' feelings and emotions often get squelched. At the same time, an abusive environment needs to be vented and requires validation and understanding. Frequently, victims need to be acclimated to a caring environment and receive support for interacting with people.

Chapter seven introduces the reader to the concept of battling DEMONS. Our nightmares and bad experiences haunt us much as demons would. So, this mnemonic provides the reader with a structure for coping and exercises to help identify strengths and weaknesses, positive and negative feelings, and stop thinking poorly. After these exercises, a guide for action helps to pass anxiety.

It would be remiss if chapter eight did not offer sources for help. Often, domestic violence leaves the victim so insecure, distrustful, and unsure of themselves that they do not know how to find help or who to ask for help. Frequently, people that the victim considered friends turn out not to keep the victim's location secret. Or the victim's fears of retaliation from the abuser cloud the judgment, thus making it difficult to choose a course of action. Then the victim resigns themselves to endure the abuse longer.

Often, we got told what we were feeling. The lists provided in the Appendix allow a person to own their feelings by identification. The grouping of the list appendix sorts the possible feelings and emotions based on the effect on self-esteem. Often people might experience and not recognize some of these feelings, especially when they receive no validation.

This book serves to guide you to a new and better life, where only the person in the mirror controls your life. Your purchase of this book begins your first step to freedom, so mark the date on your calendar and celebrate the changes to a new life. Read to learn, learn to grow, grow to enjoy.

Chapter 1

Chapter 1: Turning on the Lights

Chapter 1: Turning on the Lights

"You are incompetent!" The husband hollered at his wife angrily. "My family is coming soon. The house needs cleaning. There is no food ready. The kids are screaming. What do you do all day?" He continued berating his wife as she changed a diaper on the baby for the fifth time. She wondered why he could not help her in the home.

This scene happened every weekend of the woman's life. Slowly her husband's tone and words were eroding her confidence. She wanted to cry but knew that he would tell her to "stop being a baby and grow up," his words resounded in her head as the thought crossed her mind. She wondered how she ended up in this existence.

Does this sound familiar? Have you been on the receiving end of this scene? Maybe you have witnessed someone else living this scene. Whether this scene is personal for you or not, hundreds of women live with this treatment every day of their relationship. Often, these women yearn for freedom but cannot find the strength or courage to leave, so the gaslighting continues.

What is Gaslighting?

Gaslighting describes a psychological and emotional abuse to control and manipulate another person or group. The term got coined when psychiatrists agreed that the portrayals in the movie by the same name, Gaslight, exemplified a destructive behavior and its effects.

In one scene of the movie, Gregory (played by Charles Boyer) goes into the attic to turn on the gaslights, causing them to flicker. Paula (played by Ingrid Bergman) notices the gaslights blinking, unaware of Gregory in the attic. Later, when Paula asks Gregory why the gaslights flickered, Gregory maintains that Paula imagined the flickering, thus causing Paula to doubt her senses.

Gaslighting can be associated with brainwashing; both sets of tactics possess similar characteristics. The constant assault against a person causes the person to doubt and distrust what they know and feel to be accurate, thereby granting the assaulter power over the person. This type of psychological tactic is a highly effective control method, and anyone is susceptible to it. The abuse from gaslighting can be very destructive.

Let us review the details of Jim Jones and the Peoples Temple. Jim Jones began the racially integrated church in Indianapolis in the 1950s. As the flock grew, he moved his church to Northern California in Mendocino County. Then early in the 1970s, Jim Jones established the headquarters for the church in San Francisco and opened an additional temple in Los Angeles.

Public officials and the media favored Jim Jones by donating money to numerous charities. Jones appeared to support social equality and racial justice. His temples offered social and medical programs for impoverished individuals, including free meals, rehabilitation programs, and legal services.

Then in 1977, a magazine, New West, ran some articles that reflected poorly on Jim Jones and the People's Temple. Accompanied by more than 1,000 members of the congregation, Jones fled to Guyana to meet up with a farming extension of the church. Jones had convinced these members that the Guyana compound would be paradise. But once they got to the encampment, their passports and medications were seized.

The promised life turned into forced slavery. The communications that members would receive from the outside world received censoring. The Temple members got forced to work in the fields where mosquitos and tropical diseases plagued them. Jones had armed guards patrolling the compound's perimeter and the crops. If any member tried to escape or questioned Jones' dictates, that member would receive harsh punishments.

While in Guyana, Jim Jones obtained a jeweler's license, which entitled him to store piles of cyanide. Meanwhile, the members routinely forced into attending late-night meetings that regularly ran long suffered from lack of sleep. Often, these meetings became mandatory mock suicide drills.

Then on November 18, 1978, a delegation from the US consisting of a member of Congress, reporter, his news crew, and concerned relatives went to the farming compound in Guyana to meet with Jim Jones. The envoy received dinner and an entertainment show in their honor. Afterward, the delegation went to the local airstrip to await their plane. Jim Jones dispatched members of his congregation to kill the envoy members.

When the dispatched mercenaries returned, Jim Jones gathered his congregation and told them that soldiers would come. He added that the soldiers would torture everyone, so he gathered everyone for the encampment's radical and innovative undertaking. While everyone was convening, Jim Jones set up a tape recorder to record the monstrous event.

Jim Jones had everyone in the encampment that day drink a poisoned punch mixture. The poisoned punch that Jones ordered was made from sedatives, cyanide, and a powdered fruit juice. Armed guards surrounded the outside of the pavilion to make sure no one tried to escape. Parents and nurses were giving entire eyedropper doses of this concoction to the children. Then the adults drank the poisoned juice. This extreme occurrence demonstrates what the effect of gaslighting and brainwashing can lead a person to do.

Most women get away from their abusers alive. However, there can be an extended period for recovery from the traumatic experience of loving someone who could only love themselves. Depending on the circumstances of the relationship, a return to leading an everyday life can take years to accomplish. Occasionally, full recovery from gaslighting abuse does not happen, mainly in people who develop post-traumatic stress disorder. While this does not expose garden variety effects, it does demonstrate how easily gaslighting can lead to brainwashing and, most importantly, that gaslighting can be fatal.

Often, parents unintentionally use gaslighting to calm or quiet a child or even make a child giggle. Do you remember how an adult would pinch your nose and then act as if the tip of their thumb was your nose? It may be an innocent trick of fun but a form of gaslighting all the same.

However, the difference arises when there is the intentional use of this tactic for control or manipulation. Often, it happens so slowly that the victim does not realize what is happening. At first little things may occur, such as a prescription bottle of medicine getting hidden in a drawer under some tablecloths. When the wife discovers her prescription bottle, she asks her husband how it got into the drawer. He denies having any knowledge about the prescription bottle. The wife puts the bottle in the medicine cabinet. The next day, that same bottle of pills winds up on the window ledge in the kitchen. Once again, the husband denies any knowledge, and the wife begins to question her actions. When the husband observes the confusion of his wife, he proceeds to the next phase.

Gaslighting methods come in many forms other than the spoken word, as we can see from the above incident. This one fact is why everyone can be affected. There is no way to prevent gaslighting from happening. Although educating yourself about gaslighter's and their behaviors can help protect yourself. Once gaslighting has been identified, there are ways to handle it and recover from any harmful effects caused by it.

In the movie, Monster-In-Law, Viola invites Charlie and Kevin to the country house for a party. Viola tells Charlie that the party is a casual affair. However, when Charlie and Kevin arrive, they see that everyone is in formal attire. Viola's duplicity may have been innocent gaslighting, but it shows a gaslighting tactic. When a person starts encountering discrepancies like this from someone trusted, that person will feel disbelief and attempt shaking off the feeling that something is not proper. The victim will think that they are at fault.

A husband calls his wife from work and tells her that he will be bringing his boss home for dinner. He would like his wife to prepare a rib roast. The wife slaves all day in the kitchen, preparing this special meal for her husband's boss. When the husband comes home, no one is with him.

He asks his wife if dinner is ready and then takes his seat at the head of the dining table. The wife brings out the rib roast, and the husband then erupts with, "I called you and said I felt like trout for dinner. That does not look like trout." The wife tries to defend herself, telling him that she thought he had told her rib roast for the boss and him. The husband further berates her. The wife crumbles into tears. After dinner, the husband praises the dessert that she served to keep her off-balanced.

After five years of living in an abusive marriage, the wife has slowly sunken into a depression. The wife's appearance has changed. She no longer fixes her hair or puts on make-up. She slouches when walking, her eyes watch her feet, and she never looks anyone in the eye when talking to them. Her depression forces her into being dependent on the very person that caused the woman's depression. He completely controls her. However, she feels that her reality got turned upside down in the back of her mind.

As we can see in these scenes, the victim goes through different stages as gaslighting continues. We saw the confusion; next was the disbelief, followed by defending oneself, ending with the complete surrender of the victim's will. In chapter two, we will present more signs and symptoms of experiencing gaslighting.

The intimate knowledge that a gaslighter obtains about their victim hints to the victim's vulnerabilities, where the victim is most sensitive, how to push their victim's buttons. They use their victim against their victim. By exploiting the victim's memories, confidence, and judgment, the gaslighter can cause the victim to ponder their sanity.

Gaslighting is most used when there is an imbalance in the distribution of power in a relationship. Power imbalances in a relationship mean that this tactic is not limited to intimate relationships. Even social acquaintances can get manipulated by these toxic bullies.

Although we can instruct people about what to look for, anyone can fall prey to a gaslighter. Gaslighting may not always be intentional. Even unintentional gaslighting can generate benefits for the practitioner. The benefits may result in the practitioner eluding accountability for their actions. Or the field goal of dependency, often dependency is the primary goal of a gaslighter.

When a delivery room nurse tells you that the contractions are not that bad, a professional uses gaslighting in an attempt to calm you. When Fidel Castro launched the Mariel Boatlift, some Americans referred to the immigrants as "the dirty boat people who need to get out of this country." Or when Governor Bill Clinton announced that he had tried marijuana a couple of times during his presidential campaigning but did not inhale. Or when Exxon vehemently denied climate changes even though they had expert studies showing the contrary. As we can see, gaslighting gets practiced by the medical profession, racists, political figures, and large conglomerates. It is a skillfully used method of swaying people to see a different point of view. This point does not do the practice of gaslighting alright, and it just shows the prevalence of it in our society and how accepting we can be.

What is Trauma?

People will experience trauma when they encounter a highly stressful situation that threatens or is harmful to them. These threats or harm can affect the person physically or emotionally. However, not every person that goes through the same situation will suffer any trauma. Often, traumatized people experience a wide range of emotions immediately after an episode and over a long term. And the field of physical and emotional symptoms can be extensive.

However, trauma does not always occur immediately, so not everyone who faces threats or harm will display trauma symptoms immediately. Research has estimated that between 60-75% of North Americans will suffer a traumatic ordeal at some point during their lives. So, we need to understand the differing types of traumas. Like burns, there are varying degrees of trauma:

Acute trauma occurs after a single exposure to a stressful or dangerous event, for instance, a car accident that totals the vehicle. The driver of that car may be traumatized to the point that they refuse to drive ever again.

Chronic trauma occurs after exposure to recurring and extended periods of enduring stressful events. We can find examples of this form of trauma every day, ranging from child abuse to domestic violence and bullying. A victim of gaslighting would be a candidate for chronic trauma.

Complex trauma arises from experiencing many traumatic events. For instance, domestic violence and a car accident were the recurring abuse, then witnessing a murder, followed by three family deaths within one month. To some, this may seem like a case of bad luck. However, these many stressful events in a short time can induce complex trauma.

Vicarious trauma can also occur. This form is a secondary trauma that happens when a person is close to someone that experiences a traumatic event. An example of this would be a pipe bomb going off in the face of a friend that you were meeting for coffee.

PTSD or post-traumatic stress disorder, a debilitating condition, can happen when trauma persists or worsens weeks and months after experiencing extreme stress. War veterans often experience PTSD; however, child abuse and domestic violence survivors often experience PTSD. Once PTSD develops, it can continue for years.

PTSD can follow a stressful ordeal that causes the person to experience shock, helplessness, or fear. With a lifetime prevalence of PTSD in the United States under 10%, we can determine that most people who suffer traumatic ordeals do not develop PTSD. However, counselors tell us that females are more likely than males to suffer PTSD.

Further discussion concerning the associated signs, symptoms, and risk factors for traumas occurs in chapter five.

What is narcissism?

Narcissism is a common disorder amongst gaslighters, so there is a need to understand what the term means. The definition of narcissism tells us that this means a person who maintains excessive adoration for themselves. Commonly, a person with a narcissistic personality disorder will have an intense need for attention, awe, and approval. Narcissists are emotional, impulsive, and quick to anger. They are only concerned with how things will affect them or make them appear.

Often, gaslighters get diagnosed as narcissists, yet examining the term narcissist reveals that the narcissistic personality lacks the drive or desire for coercion. However, the twin personality to a narcissist, the Machiavellian nature, possesses the drive and desires for total control by any means possible. There can be a mixture of both personality types because of the close relation between Narcissism and Machiavellianism. There can even exist types that crossover or flip between narcissism and Machiavellian. The apparent differences between the two will determine the personality's controlling style.

A Machiavellian personality type desires wealth and power without conscience or remorse for how they get it. Even when the Machiavellian appears to be helping others, there will be a dual agenda that benefits them. They seek out others for the advantages that can be received, using these people as stepping-stones to reach a goal. They are distressed by the goodness in humans and focused on success. They view goodness as a weakness and dependence as naivety. Machiavellians stay distant from their emotions and actions.

By understanding the differences between attention-seeking and delusional or controlling and manipulative, a person becomes better equipped to cope with these types. Although, living with either style can put a strain on any relationship. Keep in mind that signs of a personality type do not appear right away. Often, they develop gradually as the relationship becomes closer. The following are typical ploys that narcissists commonly use. The narcissist will:

· During the beginning of your relationship, a narcissist frequently tells a person that they are the best thing to have ever happened. And that a whirlwind has swept them off their feet. But then things can change.

· Isolate you from family and friends since any time away from the narcissist provokes them to become unglued and steal the attention they crave.

· Narcissists tend to project feelings, actions, and opinions onto a person. So, if the narcissist considers cheating, they will accuse their partner of the action. While a person did not say this, a narcissist will use it.

· Pit a person against the world by making generalized statements, for instance, "Everyone knows that you belittle me." Words such as this one present a way for the narcissist to gain control by making you feel guilty and to keep you away from others.

· Narcissists believe that they do not need to follow the same rules. If a narcissist cheats, they will expect a person's forgiveness. However, if a person cheats, the narcissist will resort to name-

calling and questioning the person's faithful-
ness.

- Another person will never be good enough for a narcissist. Often, a narcissist will look for ways for a person to improve. Generally, they will make comments or attacks about a person's appearance.

- A narcissistic injury generally results in a verbal explosion. When a person breaks one of a narcissist's rules, that person will hear about it. Of course, once the temper tantrum has subsided, the narcissist will reconcile afterward. But each of these narcissistic-injury temper tantrums will be more explosive than the previous ones.

- Narcissists will compete over everything. If a person is hungry for a burger, the narcissist will be hungrier and want a steak. The option of succeeding against a narcissist does not exist. The narcissist must be number one at everything, from looks to intelligence to abilities.

- Narcissists demonstrate ego-syntonic behavior. In other words, they believe that it is never their fault. Everyone else in the world is the problem, not the narcissist.

- A narcissist will use derogatory or colorful terms to describe their past partners.

- Typically, the narcissist will put all the blame on the one-time partner for a failed relationship.

- Occasionally, narcissists will resort to silent treatment when they have felt slighted. They will not speak to a person to gain power and control. After all, the person has no idea what affronted the narcissist that resulted in the silence. The person may bend over backward trying to appease the narcissist.

- Often, a person's needs never get filled by a narcissist. A request for help might fall on the narcissist's deaf ears. Or the narcissist may agree to do something but then never follow through.

- Typically, there is a vast difference between a narcissist's words and actions, so pay attention.

- A narcissist takes offense quickly when a person changes their mind about plans. The narcissist will view the change as a loss of control and resort to gaslighting tactics to regain control.

- Often, narcissists will deny things that they have said or done. This tactic allows the narcissist to manipulate people.

- Frequently, narcissists are charismatic and friendly to everyone, but they can be demanding and controlling when alone with their partners.

- When a person tries to leave a relationship with a narcissist, the narcissist will attempt to win back control by using any means possible.

- Narcissists crave attention, even if it is negative attention.

- Generally, narcissists only spend money on themselves. Even when they have money, they will get the other person to pay. In this manner, a narcissist applies guilt to get someone else to spend money. Often by reminding the person about all the times in the past that the narcissist has paid.

 · The choice of gifts a narcissist gives tends to be questionable. Either the item does not apply to the recipient, or it is too extravagant to be affordable.

 · Holidays can be the worst with a narcissist since the narcissist cannot always be the center of attention.

 · Typically, narcissists will tell other people that their partner is crazy.

· When a narcissist senses that a person can no longer provide sufficient attention, the narcissist will break up with the person or drop out of sight.

After an hour, the wife finally got the children to bed. She then joined her husband in the living room in front of the TV. The wife listened to the television while she worked on a sweater that she was making. When the news program ended, the husband wordlessly rose from his chair and went to take a shower.

When the husband came out of the bathroom, the wife could smell her husband's after-shave. The husband crossed to the bedroom, where he put on one of his business suits. The puzzled woman asked where he was going this late in the night, but the man did not answer her. After checking his appearance for the fifth time, the man walked out of the door. He left without saying anything. He got into the car, then starting it, he drove away.

The puzzled woman walks over to the window and watches as the taillights disappear into the darkness. She felt bewildered at not knowing why her husband left, fearful that her husband would not be coming back, and worried that something might happen during the night. Television could not distract her feelings, so she paced the length of the house quietly so as not to wake the children.

The above scenario demonstrates how a narcissist will "punish" someone for ignoring them. The wife in the above scene had focused all her attention on the children. Bedtime routines regularly denied her husband any attention. Then when she did join her husband in the living room, the wife focused on her knitting and not her husband. Since the wife seemingly denied the husband's narcissistic-personality attention, the man decided to go out to find his spotlight.

The above story may seem insignificant all by itself. However, it does exhibit tactics employed by narcissists and gaslighters. And the tale expresses feelings and reactions that the victims often experience.

Chapter 2

Chapter 2: Shadow of Evidence

Chapter 2: Shadow of Evidence

A husband brought his wife home from the hospital. Both of them had previous marriages. She had children from her previous marriages, but he had never had children of his own.

She had been in the hospital for a hysterectomy, and her discharge instructions ordered her to bed rest for the next week. After her long battle with female problems and the surgery, she possessed no strength to quibble over bed rest. She went to the bedroom and laid down on the bed. She heard the baseball game playing on the television in the living room. Knowing that her husband was in the living room with his beer and ballgame, the woman drifted off to a dreamless sleep.

When the woman woke up, it was dark outside, and she felt disoriented about the time. She slowly rose from the bed and headed to the kitchen. She looked around and saw the light on in the kitchen. Her husband was in front of the open refrigerator.

"Hi, Hun. What are you up to?" she asked the man with his head in the refrigerator.

"Thought I would make some supper for us," he answered, "Did you rest well?" He asked as he placed a pound of ground beef and onion on the counter.

"I think so; I'm feeling a little woozy from the meds," she answered.

"I'm making tacos. Would you like some?"

"Hmmm, I might be able to eat one. I'm not hungry right now." She replied before heading to the bathroom. When she came out, her husband was still in the kitchen, stirring his meat mixture. She admired her husband's cooking skills and was relieved that she did not have to cook that evening. She headed back to the bed, where she fell back asleep.

The next time she woke up, the only visible light

was coming from the living room. She got up and walked into the living room. Her husband was sitting on the couch playing solitaire and watching the news.

"Hi."

"I saved you a plate. It is staying warm in the oven." He said without turning to look at her.

"Thank you," she said before heading to the kitchen. She took her plate from the oven and then poured a glass of milk. Then she grabbed a couple of napkins before heading into the living room with her dinner. She ate in silence as the news related the events of the day around the world. When she finished eating, she took the plate to the kitchen. She rinsed the plate and glass before setting them in the bottom of the sink to get washed.

She rejoined her husband in the living room. They quietly discussed the planning of a trip, finances, and baseball. When she was tired, she went to the bedroom for more sleep. At some point, while she slept, her husband climbed into bed with her. He slipped his arm around her and held her tight.

The following two days were uneventful, and the husband went to work like he usually did. He worked on the second shift and the factory. However, the following third day was when it began. The wife slowly regained her strength as she recovered from the surgery. After her husband left for work, she saw his tool bag on the floor bedroom closet when she grabbed her clothes.

The wife went carefully about her daily business of doing light house cleaning. The few dishes that the two of them had used for breakfast got washed. She took a break and watched a soap opera. Then while watching an afternoon game show, she dusted the living room furniture while seated on the couch.

Her husband was a good cook, but he did not know how to dust. He always used a damp dishcloth to wipe everything down, which dulled the finish on the wood furniture. She would use furniture polish to bring the shine back to the finish and protect the furniture.

When her husband came home, he quickly inspected the house before positioning himself in front of the television to watch the day's news. After the news program, he threw a pizza in the oven for dinner. They ate the pizza in front of the television. There was little for her to do after dinner, so she headed to the bedroom.

He shouted at his wife to bring him another beer when she went into the bedroom to put on her nightgown. She brought him the beer and then sat on the couch to read a book. When she finished reading a chapter, she kissed him good night and went to bed.

"Think I am calling it an early evening," she told him.

"Alright, I will be in there shortly," he said.

She was still taking her after-surgery medicines, so she fell asleep as soon as her head touched the pillow. During the middle of the night, she abruptly awakened when the bedsprings let go of the headboard. The jolt of the springs hitting the floor caused her abdomen to hurt. Awake and hurting, she went to the kitchen to get water to take a painkiller. The light was on in the living room, but her husband was not there.

She went back to the bedroom to look at what had jolted her awake. When she turned on the light, she saw that the headboard had separated from the springs. She knew that her discharge orders strictly prohibited her from lifting anything over ten pounds. She went back to the living where she laid down on the couch and turned on the television. When her husband came home, he woke her and told her to go to bed.

"I cannot; the bed broke," she told him. "I am sorry."

"What? I will look in a minute," and he went to the kitchen to grab a beer from the refrigerator. Then he set the beer on the coffee table before going to inspect the bed. Soon he returned to the living room and sat down to drink his beer. "The bed is fixed. You can go back to bed now."

"Thank you," the wife replied.

When she woke up, she noticed a little blood on her underwear. She turned on the light as she entered the bedroom and saw that the bed looked like a bed instead a wide slide. She turned off the light and crawled back onto the bed. She thought little about it since she had that surgery a week ago. She decided that she would take it easy that day instead of cleaning the house.

She knew her husband had to work overtime that night so he would be home late. She had a light dinner, then watched an hour of television before going to bed. That night was uneventful, and when she woke up, she discovered her husband asleep on the couch. He often passed out asleep on the sofa, so this was not uncommon. She woke him up so that he could get ready for work. She heard the shower turn on and then off while she sat on the couch crocheting.

"I have to pick up Dale on the way to work today," her husband told her as he headed towards the door.

"Try to wash my clothes today. I have nothing clean to wear."

"Okay, I can do that."

"I will probably be late again, so do not hold supper."

"Oh...," she responded, hoping that she hid her disappointment at another evening alone. She had planned a special dinner for that evening's meal.

He then bent over and kissed her before heading out the door. She heard his truck start up and pull out of the driveway. There was an odd sense of fear and loneliness in her that the TV could not drown out.

When she finished crocheting the row that she was working on, she rose from the couch and walked to the laundry room. Her husband had been considerate enough to set the basket of dirty clothes on top of the dryer. Out of habit, the wife checked the bedroom for more dirty clothes. She noticed the toolbox propping open the closet door.

Carefully she washed the laundry and cautiously moved the clothes to the dryer. She was mindful of the ten-pound limit that the doctor had ordered. She took several breaks throughout the day as she cleaned around the house. The clean clothes were folded and put in dresser drawers by dinner time, and then swept the floor, washed dishes, and put everything away. She had even cleaned the bathroom.

She enjoyed a light supper and worked on her crocheting in front of the television that evening. As she wearily went to bed, satisfaction crept in that she had most of her strength back. That night as she slept, the bed broke again. This time only one side of the bedsprings let go of the headboard. And once again, her husband came home to find her asleep on the couch.

He woke her up and said, "I told you that I would be late. You should not have waited for me."

"The bed broke again," she mumbled.

"I will fix it." He said as he headed out of the living room. "There, all fixed," he said when he came back to sit on the couch.

"Would you want me to make you some food to eat?" the wife asked.

"I am fine. I had a bite to eat on my way home."

"Okay. I am tired, so I am going to bed." She kissed him before going to the bedroom.

She turned on the light and saw that the bed did indeed look fixed. She walked over to the side of the bed that had fallen to examine it. The bolt that held the frame to the headboard was the only finger tight. She looked in the tool bag on the closet floor for a wrench to tighten the bolt. She found a socket that would fit on the bolt instead of the tool. She twisted the bolt tighter as much as her strength allowed her to tighten it. Then she climbed into bed, feeling confident that the bed would not fall again that night.

The next day was like any other day. Her husband went to work an hour early, and she thought that he might get off early. The rest of the day, she puttered around the house doing chores, crocheting, and reading.

During her medical leave from work, she often felt pangs of yearning to see her family, and this day was no different. Her parents lived in a state in the northeast, and her children lived in the northwest states. She was feeling alone in the world.

That night before crawling under the covers, she set the alarm so she could get up when her husband came home. She fell asleep as the radio played relaxing music. She was dreaming about walking in a summer field, a light wind blowing through her hair. A dog was running circles around her as she walked. Suddenly she was painfully jolted awake as the head of the bed collapsed, and blood gushed out of her. It felt like something had torn on the inside. She knew she needed to go to the hospital, so she called her husband at work.

He ignored that his wife was curled up in pain lying on the couch when he got home. "You best have a really good excuse for calling me at work instead of waiting until I came home. You got my pay docked for leaving early," he told her. "What happened?"

"The bed broke again," she answered, "and I am bleeding heavily. Something is not right. I need to go to the hospital."

"Okay, let me change clothes, and then I will take you. But there had better be something wrong with you." He walked into the bedroom to change his clothes. But when he saw the mattress covered with her blood, he screamed at her that they would not be able to sell the bed now.

"I am sorry," she said timidly. "I was asleep when it happened."

The hospital kept her for observation to make sure the hemorrhaging stopped. Her husband did not come to visit her the following day. And when she called home on her second day in the hospital, a woman answered the phone. Her head spun in disbelief as she hung up the phone. Had her husband been having an affair? Who was the woman that answered the phone? Why was she answering his phone? Had he been loosening the bolts on the bed?

She had not been suspicious before now, but then she remembered seeing the tool bag in the bedroom closet. Typically, her husband kept that bag on the shelf in the laundry room. Why had the bag been in the bedroom closet? She felt confused, deceived, and betrayed.

Most compassionate people will find the above scenario disconcerting. The wife was far from family and friends. And even though the husband was feigning everyday behavior, some things he was doing secretly.

As we can see by the scene above, a gaslighter's manipulation techniques are not always clear-cut. However, if a person is isolated from their family and friends, it becomes easier for an abuser to control them. So, we will discuss various techniques that get used.

· Blatantly lies to a person. For instance, the person that tells you that they are going to the store to get cigarettes. The store is only 10 minutes away, but the person is gone for four hours.
· Countering occurs when a person's memory gets

questioned. For example, "are you sure that you put your keys on the hook?"

- Withholding happens when the abuser refuses to engage in conversation. Often, they pretend not to understand. Consider this scenario, a wife asks if the husband wants to go to the movies, and he continues reading a magazine without answering the question.

- Trivializing happens when a person's feelings get belittled or disregarded. For instance, when you begin crying at a funeral and get told to be quiet.

- Denying occurs when the abuser pretends to forget events, what they said or did, or accuse someone of making things up. For example, "when did I say we would go camping this week-end?"

- Diverting happens when the abuser changes the focus of the conversation by questioning a person's credibility or sanity. Such as this scenario, during a discussion about gas light being on in the car. And the spouse replies, "are you sure? I just filled the tank yesterday."

- Stereotyping can show when the abuser intentionally mentions negative images of race, ethnicity, gender, sexual orientation, nationality, or age. For instance, the wife tells the husband about a car backing into her at the store, and the husband replies, "if you were not a woman driver that would not have happen."

- They tell a person that their family and friends

are talking about them behind their backs. For example, "you know your sister told my brother about your habit of knocking on wood to prevent being jinxed. They think you are crazy!"

· They hide things from a person and then deny knowing anything about the missing object. Such as this scenario, a wife habitually places her keys on a shelf next to the door. While she gets ready to go out, the husband puts her keys in the freezer when he grabs a beer. When she discovers her keys missing, she asks if he has seen them, and he says, "nope, guess you will have to stay home."

· Insists that the person went somewhere that they have never been. For instance, a husband states, "remember we went to that lake to go skinny dipping when you were 17," but you know you have never been to that lake, let alone skinny dipping with your husband.

· Insists that the person never went somewhere that they know they have been. For example, you are telling friends about a concert the two of you saw, and your husband says, "you were not with me at that concert."

· They tell a person negative things concerning the person's children, family, or friends. Such as this scenario, "no wonder your kids are thieves, they take after their father."

· Falsely gossips about you to friends that will back the abuser. For instance, you hear your partner talking to one of their friends, and they tell the friend, "She shoplifts, so I cannot take her anywhere."

· They tell a person what that person is thinking or feeling, even though wrong. For example, "you know you think that so and so is stupid for marrying that girl."

· They shift the blame to the target. Such as this scenario, "if you did not walk so loudly, I would not have a headache" as you look at the empty case of beer left on the table.

· Displays mood swings. For instance, when a husband laughs at a funny story that his wife tells him. Then she goes into the kitchen to check on dinner and turns around to leave the kitchen, just as the husband grabs her arms and shakes her, screaming, "what did you do with the TV remote?"

· They display secretive behavior. For example, the wife is getting the children ready to go out for the day when she hears the front door slam close. She hurried to the window to look outside. She saw that the car was gone, so she decided to play with the kids in the yard. Her husband walks in with a bag in his hand that he brings to the bedroom six hours later. "Where were you?" She asks. "Out." He replies. "Where is the station wagon?" she asked. "Traded it." He answers

· Shows concern or gets involved when the target

participates in a situation that the gaslighter wants to control. Such as this example "Let me show you how to sweep so you do not work so vigorously. Work smarter, not harder."

· Acts kind but persuasive, for instance, "I will take you to that restaurant that you like if you will be my designated driver tonight."

· Frequently, they resort to intimidation and threats. For example, a wife is sitting on a couch with her husband. Suddenly, he pulls a 45 caliber gun out of the cushions and waves it in her face yelling, "if your kids ever come around here again, I will kill them and you."

· Often uses name-calling such as this scenario, "You stupid douchebag, you left my tools out!" when a husband finds a screwdriver on the kitchen counter.

· Frequently argues about minor details; for instance, a husband watches his wife folding laundry. When she grabs a matching pair of socks, he watches her ball the socks and tells her that is the wrong way of folding socks. He then shows her how to pull the sock cuff down to keep the pair together.

Sheila got ready for her date with Ray. It was their first date, and Sheila had purchased a special outfit for it. She looked in the dressing mirror, adjusted the collar on her top, and gave herself a nod of approval.

Sheila twisted her hair into a bun and then applied her evening make-up. Then she chose a sweater from the closet and grabbed her purse before going into the living room, where she left the items on the sofa.

Sheila was rinsing out her coffeepot when she heard a knock on her apartment door. She knew that it should be Ray showing up. As Sheila headed towards the front door, she glanced around the apartment to ensure that everything was where it belonged.

"Hi," she said as she opened the door. "Come on in." She welcomed Ray into the apartment with a smile.

"Hi. I bought you something!" Ray said as he walked into the apartment with his hands behind his back. He moved his hands to the front to show Sheila a teddy bear. "I have a story about this."

Sheila took the adorable bear and listened while Ray related his story about the bear and the shopkeeper. When Ray finished telling Sheila the adventure of getting the bear, Sheila waited for the man to finish the story before setting the toy down. She was unsure why Ray had told her, but she placed the bear on the sofa and grabbed her sweater and evening bag.

"I thought we would eat at that new restaurant La Croix Cuivre before going to the show."

"Sounds good." Sheila responded. She knew that the downtown merchants were hosting a blues festival this weekend. She hoped that they would be able to find parking downtown. The rest of the way to the restaurant, Sheila and Ray talked about the architecture in the historic district.

La Croix Cuivre served an eclectic nouvelle cuisine. Sheila looked down at the "Poisson avec asperges au fromage" that the waiter placed in front of her. The chef had put a little piece of fish on top of a scoop of wild rice. On the opposite side of the plate rested six spears of asparagus with enough cheese sauce to touch the plate. The middle of the dish was white, vacant of any food or sauce touching. Sheila decided that after she returned home, she would be able to have a filling snack.

The rest of the evening was a pleasant change from sitting at home listening to music. Ray walked Sheila to her apartment door and said good night to her. Once inside, Sheila picked up the teddy bear and took it to her closet. Looking at the bear before placing it on a shelf, Sheila realized that she had no idea what to do with it.

The next day, a bouquet arrived at Sheila's workplace. That evening, Ray phoned while Sheila cleaned up after supper. They planned to go out for dinner in three days.

Ray took Sheila to the Grecian Urn, where they sat out on the patio while eating. This time the meal was overflowing on the plates. Sheila was full before everything had disappeared from her plate. Since both had to work the next day, they decided to make it an early evening.

When they got to Sheila's apartment, she asked Ray in for a cup of coffee. They talked for 30 minutes while drinking coffee, and then Ray headed to the door.

"Thanks for the coffee and the company at dinner." Ray said.

"I had a nice time," Sheila told him.

"Well, I have an early day tomorrow." Ray told her.

"Yeah, I must work late tomorrow."

"Well, we will get together soon." Ray opened up the door, took two steps out, and then suddenly, he turned around to add, "Before I can see you again, you will need to change."

"Change?" Sheila asked, perplexed.

"You need to fix your nose." Ray said flat out. "And

get caps on your teeth and do something with your hair." Then he walked out the door.

Sheila had been too astounded to respond. That night and the next day, she kept wondering what was wrong with her nose? Why did she need caps on her teeth? What was wrong with her hair? Who did he think he was to say those things to her?

Gaslighting tactics will effectively whittle away a person's self-esteem, confidence, and will. Any efforts to make someone doubt themselves constitute gaslighting and abuse. Typically, the victim undergoes:

- No longer feeling like the person they once were
- Suffer more anxiety and less confidence than they used to possess
- Frequently wonders if they are overly sensitive
- Believe everything they do comes out wrong
- Ruminate over perceived character flaws
- Believes they hold the blame when anything goes wrong
- Constantly apologizes for every little thing
- Know that something is not right, but cannot identify what is wrong
- Frequently questions the appropriateness of what they said to the abuser
- Always makes excuses for the abuser's behavior

- Staying silent instead of voicing an opinion
- Avoids giving information to friends and family about the abuser to prevent confrontations
- Feels isolated or distanced from family and friends
- Finds it increasingly more difficult to make simple decisions
- Feel on the edge and lack self-esteem
- Suffers from hopelessness and takes little pleasure in favored activities
- Feel confused, unintelligent, inadequate, insane, and repeat these words to yourself
- Constantly second-guessing themselves
- Withdraws and becomes unsociable
- Lies to family and friends to dodge dreaming up excuses for the abuser
- Disappointed in who you have become
- Worry that you are what the abuser tells you that you are
- Possess a sense of impending doom
- Feels joyless, worthless, or incompetent
- Believe that others are disappointed in you.
- Lack of understanding why you are not happier in life.
- Wears a person down slowly
- Start telling lies to avoid put-downs and reality twists
- Lack of acceptance, validation, and understanding

- Feel fuzzy about own thoughts, feelings, or beliefs
- Wonder if you are good enough as a partner
- Feel disconnected or out of touch from reality
- Think twice before bringing up specific innocent topics of conversation
- Run through a mental checklist of the events of the day to steel yourself before your partner gets home
- Possess the feeling that you were a different person once – more self-assured, more vibrant, more easy-going

If a person frequently relates to five or more of these feelings, they should re-examine their relationship for gaslighting. These feelings can indicate a mental health concern, such as a generalized anxiety disorder or a seasonal depression. We advise anyone who experiences any type of abuse to seek help from a reputable counselor, therapist, psychologist, or psychiatrist.

Gaslighters master the ability to zero in on sensitivities and vulnerabilities so they can push their victim's buttons. This ability will leave their victim doubting themselves, their memories, judgment, and even their sanity. This double-edged sword that the callous gaslighter swings around can also lead to their victim experiencing trauma or mental illness from the treatment.

Abusers will employ the following or similar phrases to accomplish their manipulation of a victim:

- "You never remember things."
- "Are you sure?"
- "What are you talking about?"
- "Stop trying to confuse me."
- "You are just overreacting."
- "Look at you, no wonder I do not want to come home."
- "Why blow this out of proportion?"
- "You are making that up."
- "You are too sensitive."
- "You are crazy."
- "It is no big deal."
- "Stop talking crazy."
- "You act crazy."
- "Oh, come on now, I never said that."
- "You are just paranoid."
- "Who gave you such a crazy idea?"
- "Do you think a woman can lift that?"
- "Oh, snap, now you are going to feel sorry for yourself."
- "Didn't you know that your family thinks that you are going crazy?"
- "I never said that."

- "What are you talking about?"
- "Did you lose your purse again?"
- "You are always losing things!"
- "You never went there with me, and I should know!"
- "You never should have had children!"
- "You are getting angry over a little thing like this!"
- "You are always so angry; no wonder we have problems."
- "I only married you because I was drunk!"
- "You always make things up to confuse me."
- "That never happened!"
- "You know I love you and that I would never hurt you."
- "You only feel that way because you are so insecure."
- "You have no sense of humor!"
- "I was just joking / kidding!"
- "You are imagining things."
- "You are being dramatic,"
- "You are being hysterical."
- "There is not a pattern."
- "You are seeing things that are not there."
- "Do not get so worked up."
- "There you go again."
- "You are so ungrateful."
- "I will not go through this again with you."
- "Why should I believe you when no one else does?"

- "You need to see a psychiatrist."
- "Did you hear that garbage in your therapy session today?"
- "Do you have to walk like that?"
- "I cannot stand the sound of your voice."

If three or more of these phrases sound familiar or get repeated frequently, a person needs to consider that they are a subject of gaslighting. At the same time, a person does need to consider the context in which a phrase gets stated. These phrases rarely get heard in healthy relationships where both partners are concerned about the other partner's feelings and interests.

Frequently, gaslighters will begin with the truth about something sensitive for a person to get to that person. And then typically, gaslighting occurs gradually and goes through stages. The sequence of gaslighting stages follows the ones for grief. In that, they do not need to happen in order sequentially. The person can jump around the different steps. An appropriate mnemonic acronym to remember the gaslighting stages: POTLUCK.

- Pinocchio for the lies and exaggerations of a gaslighter

)ver and over for the repetitiveness of a
gaslighter's deceit
- Turn up the heat for the escalation in attacks
  that happens when a gaslighter gets confronted
- Lessen for the weakening of a person's will by
  the gaslighter
- Union for the codependent relationship that
  gets formed with a gaslighter.
- Clinging for the false hope gaslighters employ to
  keep a person hooked
- Kaiser for the gaslighter's goal of domination
  and control

Since a gaslighter's actions and words can be un-
predictable, potluck seems to be an appropriate term
to describe what a person goes through with this type
of abuser.

Meanwhile, a victim subjected to gaslighting and
losing their sense of resolve can go through a grief-
like cycle every step of the way to complete submission. The main stages of the grief cycle are rejection,
outrage, down-hearted, haggling, resignation. However, for the victim of a gaslighter, the grief-like
process turns into:

- Disbelief that they receive this treatment
- Anger at being subjected to being gaslit

- Begging for validation of feelings and freedom from the gaslighting
- Depression when their hope vanishes
- Acquiescence when they submit entirely control to the gaslighter

This grief-like cycle can go on for years, even after the victim leaves the relationship.

Chapter 3: Puppeteer Types

Chapter 3: Puppeteer Types

While it is not possible to sit in an outdoor café and point out each gaslighter walking past on the street, gaslighters have some traits in common. Typically, men are gaslighters, not women. Experts have argued that women get conditioned to seek relationships and connections while men seek power. This conditioning leaves women vulnerable to exploitation. However, gaslighting does not discriminate against gender, race, age, intelligence, orientation, or wisdom.

Gaslighters possess a chameleon duality of charisma and innocuousness, switching to arrogant and controlling. They can be exceedingly persuasive with their charismatic ways or intimidating when they show their arrogant side. Or they can be a sly fox that weasels information from their victims to use that information for coercion. Often, they have an intense need to control their life by making others dependent on them. The previous statement explains why people with certain personality disorders or character flaws employ gaslighting techniques to achieve a goal.

People who gaslight typically have an authoritarian type of personality. This rigid person tends to think in black and white, and there is no flexibility for them. Something is either 100% right or 100% wrong; there is no in-between or gray area for this type of person. Often these people believe that strength of character equals effectively controlling their inferiors. Usually, these characteristics identify the authoritarian personality:

- Unquestioning allegiance t traditional beliefs about right and wrong
- An adverse opinion about humanity in general
- Honor and compliance to recognized authority
- Commitment to forceful administration with steadfast sovereignty
- Creed for the offensive against those who are different or hold differing beliefs
- Defiance on new or innovative ideas
- A doctrine of simple answers and disputes
- A habit of casting their inadequate feelings, fears, and anger on others, often a scapegoat group

· A fixation with sex and violence

Some gaslighters suffer from a personality disorder, such as antisocial personality disorder, where a person has an insatiable desire to control people and deep-seated anxieties. The mental health condition known as antisocial personality disorder displays a pattern of manipulation, exploitation, or violation of rights for other people over a long period. Often this behavior type is criminal. Usually, these types of people will do the following:

· Act rashly
· Break the law
· Experience failing to meet money, work, or social duties
· Lie, con, and exploit others
· Fight or assault others
· Not care about anyone's safety, including theirs
· Abuse alcohol or drugs
· Never exhibit remorse after hurting someone

Or they have an ego-syntonic personality. The person is committed to believing that they do not own the problem and everyone else causes the issues. Often ego gets described as the internal voice of reason. Syntonic refers to behaviors displayed congruent with a person's values and self-image as determined by the ego. So, this rigid and inflexible personality does and says things that agree with the ego's values, goals, and self-mage.

A dark, ruthless, and vicious personality type known as the Machiavellian uses manipulative tactics so effectively that it is difficult to recognize this personality. The term received the name after the diplomat, political theorist, and author of a political treatise entitled, The Prince, Niccolo Machiavelli. There are signs which can identify a Machiavellian personality.

- Power obsession
- A cynical view of the world
- A self-centered callous desire to subjugate
- Enthusiasm to exploit others
- Gaslighting architect

Another type of disorder where people often employ gaslighting is known as narcissistic personality disorder. This disorder is where people believe that they are the most crucial person in the world. These people are self-absorbed and unempathetic. They lack the ability or interest to understand what someone else experiences or feels. They crave attention and admiration, often demanding it. Their views of themselves, their life, and future are grandiose. And they are known to use manipulation to achieve personal goals. A person with this disorder can be recognized by:

· Inflated sense of self that they project
· Exaggerating their successes, awards, and achievements
· Expect special treatment, at times demanding it
· Get angry when criticized
· Use other people for personal gain
· Are highly critical of other people
· Can quickly become envious

Typically, addicts of any type (alcohol, drugs, sex, etc.) often resort to gaslighting techniques when confronted about their addiction. The effects of drugs and alcohol can warp a person's character, self-image, and values. Subconsciously addicts feel out of control, so they have a strong need to control the world around them. Through gaslighting, an addict finds that they can find or create an "enabler," a person that makes it easier for the addict to avoid confronting their addiction.

In psychology, there is not a disorder described as an addictive personality. However, it is well known that if a person is addicted to one thing, they are more susceptible to other addictions. Although, some common personality traits for addicts are:

- A love for excitement, i.e., sexual flings, driving fast, taking risks
- Snap decisions or impulsivity
- Their need to achieve the same thrill as the first time they felt the rush. A tolerance builds, so they need to do more to get the same high.
- Unable to quit

And finally, it is common for bullies and pimps to use intimidation through gaslighting their targets. These sorts of people take advantage of people who are smaller, weaker, or in some other way disadvantaged and vulnerable. Bullies will often exhibit the following behaviors:

- Controlling rather than leading
- Impulsiveness
- Issues with managing anger
- Bouts of frustration and feeling annoyed
- Difficulty following rules
- Lack of empathy, unsympathetic about the needs and desires of others
- Little or no respect for authority
- Blames the victim for actions

- Physically stronger than others
- Regards violence in a positive way
- They may mistakenly identify fear as popularity

As we can see, most of these disorders get listed as "personality" disorders. There are other disorders that a person can be diagnosed with, such as a mood disorder or a behavior disorder. We will need to clarify the difference between personality, mood, and behavior disorders to fully comprehend the issue at hand.

A personality disorder denotes rigid and unhealthy thought patterns or behavioral patterns. A narcissistic personality disorder is a prime example of personality disorder. The following symptoms commonly characterize personality disorders:

- Fragile self-image
- Unstable relationships
- Suicidal behavior
- Impulsive behavior
- Extreme mood swings

Mood disorders denote inconsistent emotional state or mood for an individual's given circumstances. Major depression and bipolar disorder are well-known examples of mood disorders. The following symptoms commonly characterize mood disorders:

- Fatigue
- Sadness
- Changes in appetite
- Irritability
- Concentration difficulties

Personality disorders and mood disorders have similar characteristics and can easily get misdiagnosed. However, a person with a personality disorder will have difficulty interacting with others due to being fundamentally different. And a person with a mood disorder can interact with others as healthy people do during periods outside of their mood shifts to the extremes in sadness or happiness.

Behavior disorders are not limited to children; adults suffer from them also. Addictive behaviors such as alcoholism, drug abuse, and gambling are all behavior disorders. Obsessive-compulsive disorder is another lifelong disorder. All these behaviors and other behavior disorders get identified as being harmful or disruptive to oneself and others.

There are many personality disorders, other than a narcissistic personality disorder, that may employ gaslighting, such as:

- Borderline personality
- Schizophrenia
- Histrionic personality
- Psychopath
- Sociopath
- Avoidant personality (passive-aggressive)
- Obsessive-compulsive personality
- Dissociative personality
- Codependent personality

The imbalance of power in relationships creates the common thread that flows through all these different personality types. This imbalance of power creates feelings of a lack of control and stability in these people's lives. And the only way to control their lives often becomes gaslighting.

Commonly, a woman dreams of Prince Charming coming to marry her and settle down within a little white cottage. Before a date, a woman will apply make-up to her face and put on clothes to make her more appealing or sensuous to her date. At the end of the evening, when her date drops her off at the door, they kiss. The woman sees that her date does not turn into a frog, so she dates this prince. This happy couple moves in together, and the woman discovers that she has a toad for a partner.

Movies, books, magazines, and television have

demonstrated the ideal romantic partner or a caring friend. Hence, people often try to meet these standards. Generally, for a woman, those standards are:

· Generous
· Funny
· Attentive
· Wise
· Considerate
· Chivalrous
· Compassionate

And some women will stress that the person must be wealthy. But they will settle for the listed characteristics. Men often look for their ideal mate by appearances before substance. And when a woman drastically alters her appearance to attract a man, she demonstrates a lack of self-esteem. Let us consider the following experience.

A cute woman accepts a date with a man that she had never been out with before. They go out to dinner at an elegant nouvelle cuisine restaurant. They then go to see a stage production before taking her home for the night. The next day, he sends her flowers. The following day he calls her for another date.

For the next date, the woman purchases a new outfit to wear, fixes her hair, and applies make-up; nothing different or unique from any other date. When she opens the door to let her date in, he hands her a teddy bear. And tells her a sentimental story about the bear. They then go out to eat and have a pleasant time. However, the man tells her that she would have to have plastic surgery before going out again on the way home. He feels that her nose and ears need correcting. This statement took the woman back and left her feeling dazed and confused.

Why had the man asked her out in the first place? Didn't they have a pleasant date? What's wrong with my ears? What's wrong with my nose? All these thoughts danced in the woman's head. Then when they arrived back at her apartment, she warmly thanked the man for the date but did not invite him into the apartment. She had decided that there was something wrong with the man and that she would be better off without him in her life.

Generally, a person's world gets shaped by their upbringing. If they were subjected to any abuse and never recovered from it, the effects of that abuse will bubble out. For some, it comes out as gaslighting.

Typically, people do not go out looking for a gaslighter. However, specific characteristics can be associated with some people that seem to attract gaslighters. These characteristics are:

- Previous experience with abuse
- Codependency issues
- Addiction problems
- Low self-esteem
- People pleasing
- Insecurity
- Loneliness

In the previous story, we saw how someone could be preyed on if they possessed any of the above characteristics. However, no one is immune to a gaslighter. And once a person submits to gaslighting, it can be challenging to get out from under control. But there are some techniques and skills that can be useful to stop gaslighting. Here are some phrasing examples for any instance of gaslighting:

- If you continue talking like this to me, I will not respond.
- I hear what you are saying, and that is not my experience.
- I am walking away from this conversation.
- We distinctly remember things differently.
- I will gladly talk with you about [X and Y]; however, I am not talking about [Z].

· I am not interested in debating over the incident with you.

Often our confidence in finding our romantic partner casts aside our sensibility to find a good person. If we set our eyes on a Prince Charming or Lady Guinevere, we will find the perception of them. Perception becomes our fantasy of an ideal outcome if we allow it.

Centuries ago, in a different world, the custom of chaperoning a couple during courtship provided families with an opportunity to watch out for the couple's best interests. Nowadays, friends watch a date from a nearby stool or chair, waiting for an agreed-upon sign for rescue. Our friends allow us to weigh a person's merits. And when we know what values will make a good mate, we will find our happiness. The lists in this chapter provided an insight into the type of person that would not make a good mate.

However, we can still get fooled by our perceptions. The natural charisma and intelligence coupled with keen insight and salesmanship form the foundation of this type of insidious abuser, and they learn to misuse their talents. These physical traits often enable the abusers to deceive law enforcement officials that require physical proof for evidence. So, it becomes crucial for people to be vigilant against these predators.

Vigilance begins with education. This chapter provided the personality types that employ gaslighting methods. And the kind of person that often attracts abusive partners. The next chapter offers a closer look at how these individuals behave and what lines they say.

Chapter 4

Chapter 4: Taking Off the Blinders

Chapter 4: Taking Off the Blinders

Some of the tactics that gaslighters often use got demonstrated at the beginning of this book. However, those are not the only techniques. We will look at most of the standard methods used to gain and maintain control over a target. These methods, strategies, and tactics seem innocent enough when advertisers or marketing campaigns apply them to a product. However, manipulation of another person as the foundation and benefit of one's ego should be despised. This type of disrespect for another person establishes the fundamentals for criminals.

Trivialize how you feel: "Why are you crying? You know you did not love your sister?" Trivializing happens when an abuser belittles or ignores their victim's feelings. Often the abuser will accuse the victim of overreacting or being too sensitive.

Intimating that people are bad-mouthing you: "You know your friend, Sarah. She is telling everyone that you stole her necklace." The abuser implies that someone the victim trusts goes around vilifying the victim. This tactic gets employed to isolate the victim, so only the abuser gains sole propriety of the victim's trust.

Tell you something and then later deny it: "I never said that I would deposit my paycheck into the bank account. When did I say that? Now we will have to pay insufficient fees!" Denial occurs when the abuser pretends to forget events, how they happened, having said something, or done something. They will often accuse the victim of making things up or hallucinating. The more a victim questions their reality, the more they start to accept the abuser's version of reality.

Insisting that you were somewhere, even though it is not valid: "Sure, you remember we went to that outdoor concert on the lake. And we got those sun visors. You must remember those visors!?" A practical method for abusers to interject doubt, reshape their victim's memories, and create thought confusion.

Diverting happens when the abuser quickly changes the conversation topic and questions the victim's credibility. Many people do this naturally when they do not want to discuss sensitive matters. However, for a gaslighter, this critical tool frees them to act as they desire without any repercussions for their actions.

A gaslighter may feign innocence and blame their victim for creating all the problems in a relationship. "You think I caused this mess? You started it with your nagging." A method for transferring responsibility that acts to free the abuser from guilt, often weighing the victim down with guilt.

Hiding objects from you and then denying knowledge: "You always are losing your keys. It is amazing how you function." This maneuver creates self-doubt in a person or their memories.

Sometimes, abusers resort to negative stereotypes of a person's gender, race, ethnicity, sexuality, nationality, or age to manipulate a person. "That is too much car for a woman to handle. You must be crazy to consider buying it." Typically, negative stereotyping gets applied when the abuser senses defiance from a victim. Often this method provides a dual attack on the victim.

Frequently, a gaslighter will withhold their attention by refusing to listen or claiming not to understand. This tactic blocks the validation of feelings and creates a barrier of isolation. Typically, when a person encounters a lack of assurance, their self-worth decreases. The effect of this tactic results in questions such as "why me?"

Lying is the crux of the gaslighter's abilities. Blatantly lying to their victim helps a gaslighter to keep their victim unsure of reality. And the gaslighter often tells the victim that everyone else lies to the victim, that the abuser is the only one telling the truth. The success of this tactic comes when the victim turns to the abuser for "true" information.

"You never should have had those kids." Gaslighters will attack the foundation and soul of a person's being. And using what is dear to a person is the most effective way to get to that person.

Gaslighters wear their victims down gradually with a snide comment here and a lie there, a fib here, and a slam there. After a while, the gaslighter increases the frequency of their attacks on your esteem. The challenge for the gaslighter is like pushing a boulder up a hill. The more the boulder erodes, the easier and quicker the push is uphill. The ultimate reward for any gaslighter to strive for - the power of control.

"I will just have a doughnut and coffee for breakfast." But then you watch a gaslighter eat eggs, bacon, sausage links, hash browns, and orange juice along with the doughnut and coffee. Many times, a gaslighter's words are empty air; their actions will speak clearer.

Gaslighters are known to accuse their victims of the same activities in which a gaslighter participates. For instance, if the abuser has an affair, they will blame their victim for an extramarital fling. They project their actions on their victim. This distraction forces the victim to defend themselves and not question the abuser's behavior.

Typically, any pleasantries that a gaslighter uses should cast suspicion on their motives.

Occasionally, an abuser will compliment or praise their victim on something that has been said or done. This moment of kindness causes the victim to think that the abuser has changed. An abuser rarely shifts their attitudes.

Gaslighters are perceptive about people's security needs of fitting in and a support system. They use this knowledge to gain an individual's trust at first by offering understanding and comfort. After a bit, they begin to work on the side to disrupt a person's comfort and support systems by keeping a person confused and questioning reality.

The keen insights that a gaslighter possesses allow them to identify the people that will support them no matter what they do. Then they manipulate these people to stand against their victims. Bear in mind that anything stated by this abuser will often be untrue. These people are consistently weaving a web of deceit. If an abuser can isolate a victim, they can control that individual.

Often a gaslighter convinces other people that the victim is crazy or prone to hysteria and exaggerations. This sabotage of their victim's stability establishes a reason for people to disregard anything the victim tells them. A gaslighter that gains support from family and friends accomplishes a significant coup for an abuser as it offers them protection to do as they want.

Gaslighting is not a character trait that people have when they are born. It is a learned skill. Usually, a gaslighter witnessed or felt the effects of it. They know how powerful and valuable the craft's capabilities can be from observing or feeling the effects. Then they practice using the techniques until they can adeptly use them. Frequently, beginning during childhood when a victim possesses something that the future abuser desires.

Manipulation starts as a strategy for regulating a person's behaviors. However, gaslighters exploit the process for their benefit and may not be conscious of what they do. This statement does not excuse the actions or defend an abuser. The information merely provides some understanding about gaslighting. Some

gaslighters obtained the lousy habit from past relationships and may be able to break the bad habit.
However, changing a pattern, whether good or bad, is
not an easy task. There is no guarantee that one specific gaslighter will get altered.

As we can see, gaslighting techniques come in different forms, but these techniques effectively disarm
an individual and create doubt. Gaslighters are sneaky,
patient, and sly. But these traits rarely get publicly
displayed. Often, abusers possess an above-average
intelligence that they hide from ridicule. This belief
that intelligence draws negative feedback carries over
from playground teasing. However, the evidence of
abuse becomes apparent after the frequency of attacks becomes an everyday event. And the gradual-
ness of these attacks makes it hard to determine any
abuse occurring.

Publicly, a gaslighter will appear to be friendly and
confident. Yet often, what victims hear in private can
be common phrases such as these.

- Stop being so sensitive. You are too soft-
hearted!
- You are just overly sensitive.
- You are crazy.
- You are just paranoid.
- Stop being crazy!
- You have an active imagination.

- It is not a big deal.
- I do not know why you are making such a big deal about this!
- You are overreacting.
- Cut the drama!
- I was joking!
- I was kidding!
- You are making that up.
- Do not get so worked up.
- That never happened.
- We never went there.
- We never did that.
- You never remember things clearly.
- Pattern? There is no pattern.
- You see something that is not there.
- Stop being hysterical!
- You are hysterical.
- You make me laugh.
- I will not go through this again!
- You are trying to confuse me.
- There you go again; you do not appreciate anything that I do.
- You are wrong, and you never remember things.
- Stop lying!
- Who gave you that crazy idea, your friends?
- You are blowing everything out of proportion!
- It is all in your head.
- You are insecure.
- Stop being so insecure.
- You have no sense of humor.

- I cannot handle your insecurity!
- Messing up is the reason why I cannot trust you!
- You are too emotional about this!
- Forgetting is the reason why I do not put faith in you!
- I do not know what you are saying.
- You are making stuff up, as usual.
- There you go again, diving into the deep end.
- Why should I believe you? No one else does?
- Nobody believes a word you say; why should I?
- Oh, come on, I would never say anything like that.
- Oh, come on, I never said that!

If you hear three or more of the above phrases regularly, someone may be gaslighting you! If you know someone who experiences this type of abuse, talk with them about gaslighting or give them a copy of this book.

Gaslighters often partake in secretive behaviors, such as spending a long time in the bathroom, switching out medications, and flushing the prescribed medicine. Or when they go into a bedroom to change clothes but loosen the bolts holding the bed together. And then they come out wearing the same clothes. The abuser loses their edge of control when victims can prepare a defense against an assault. So, the secrecy of plans and actions becomes necessary for their continued domination.

Frequently, gaslighters are prone to mood swings. For instance, when you speak with them about setting the alarm panel. Your partner asks how to use the alarm. You explain there is a 30-second delay when they program the alarm. They need to be prepared to leave when they enter the number sequence and press the "Away" button, then go out the door. And your partner screams that the number sequence is too hard to remember and storms off. These mood swings occur naturally, but the frequency of mood swings increases when the abuser withdraws from recreational substances.

Frequently, gaslighters will use intimidation and threats to control a person. For instance, waving a pistol in your face as they tell you that a specific person can no longer come into the house. Often, abusers declare boundaries and rules when they use intimidation and threats.

Name-calling undermines a person's self-worth and implies inferiority in status. Often this juvenile tactic suggests that the abuser feels fear or hurt. For example, "Heifers should not wear hats." when you ask how a new hat looks.

Gaslighters are known to argue about minor details. These petty detail arguments reflect a perceived threat to the abuser's domain. For example, does the roll of toilet paper spin towards the wall or away from the wall. Some people consider these as signs of obsessive-compulsive personalities.

Gaslighters do have a charming side to themselves occasionally. For instance, their parents are visiting for the weekend, and while you are talking with his mother, he pours more coffee for everyone. When he returns, he asks his mother if she would like some cookies. After she answers, then he turns to you and says, "would you go get the cookies?" as he gives you one of his stern looks. Or take the case of the gaslighter returning home after disappearing to cool down from an argument and brings home a puppy for you as a means of an apology.

Please note in each of the above scenarios, the gaslighter has exhibited his emotional control by being concerned, involved, persuasive, and kind. He was concerned and interested in front of his parents to contradict any negative statements that you might make about him. The puppy scene was a play on your emotions to persuade forgiveness from you without speaking an apology. The gaslighter subtly maintained control.

As we can see, gaslighters create chaos through different techniques and methods, some of which get used in advertising campaigns. For instance, the ads that show beautiful blonde females in daisy dukes admiring a sports car. The ad implies that if you own the vehicle, you will get the woman. Implications such as this can quickly progress into creative manipulations, especially for someone familiar with the outcomes of manipulation. Often these people experienced violations of their personal space and typically established warped comfort boundaries.

Gaslighters and abusers typically contain their feelings and emotions within the innermost boundary. They rarely allow anyone to see this part of them. The area surrounding the innermost area forms the abuser's needs and self-fulfillment area. The abusers keep intimate relationships in this area since these relationships need control. The outermost region of an abusive person's personal space portrays what they desire the world to see. This division for a private sphere for gaslighters and abusers rarely reveals itself until the manipulator allows it.

So, it becomes necessary to establish guidelines concerning our comfort zone boundaries. And when we feel our boundaries get crossed or violated, we need to defend the borders by speaking out courageously. So many people become afraid of asserting their ideals lest they become ostracized from the crowd that society creates opportunities for abuse. We need to remember the creed of treating everyone (including ourselves) the way we want treatment.

When we follow this creed, we can quickly determine the type of people that we should befriend.

Chapter 5: Lighting Fallout

Chapter 5: Lighting Fallout

Severing the strings of the puppet master may not be as easy as the snapping of a fishing line. After being a prisoner for a significant portion of a person's life, the idea of freedom sounds enticing. But how to achieve it can be daunting. We will examine how to gain freedom physically. However, a person cannot live free unless they have shed the veneer that the puppet master used to encase them gradually. So, we will examine breaking free emotionally and mentally.

Typically, an abuser will not allow their victim to walk away. Abusers need their victims for a daily dose of feeling powerful and in control. Without this feeling of power, abusive individuals often lack the confidence to function in public. They are like an addict going cold turkey from their substance of choice. A natural fear and panic set in as withdrawal gets felt for the abuser. The abuser will cast various gaslighting and guilt techniques to regain control. When these methods fail, begging and bargaining often occur. Then the silence typically indicates devising a new strategy for management. As we can see, the victim needs to fortify their determination to leave and mask the secret.

The children knew that Emily had taken care of preparing the box to take to Ruth. The children watched as their mother packed clothes and toys into the package along with a pouch of papers. Then more outfits from the dryer found a place on top. Finally, their mother closed the box, and she gathered the children in the bedroom. She explained that she would take the package to Ruth and then come home with a treat in hushed tones. Eyes widened as the children wondered what treat their mother would bring home.

Emily told Jack that she needed to go into town to buy some breakfast for the family. Then she headed out to the car with the box. As she drove up the hill towards town, she felt a sense of relief wash over her with the knowledge that soon they would be free. Emily dropped the box off at Ruth's and agreed on a secret word for an emergency.

After leaving Ruth's house, Emily stopped at the grocery store on the way home. She bought milk, eggs, and pastries for the weekend's breakfast. On the drive home, Emily reviewed the escape plans. She still needed to figure out how to get the children out safely.

Emily slowed the car to scan the property around the house for a mental map. Then parking the car, Emily checked the neighboring yards on the hill. Her brain processed the calculations of the feasibility for the success of various plans. Emily's determination strove to develop the escape route.

Inside the house, Emily placed everyone's breakfast on the dining table. She then took a cup of coffee into the bedroom and put it on the night table. Emily turned to walk out of the room; a hand shot out from under the covers and forcefully grabbed her wrist, yanking her back.

"Keep those brats quiet!" Jack grunted from under the covers. The hand released her wrist.

"They are just playing."

"Keep them quiet!" Jack growled.

"Breakfast is on the table." Emily replied and adeptly moved out of range of the bed. As she walked to the dining room, she pondered how to keep four young children quiet while playing in the house.

Emily and the children sat around the dining room table eating breakfast when Jack stormed out of the bedroom. He glared at Emily as he headed to the bathroom. Emily hurried the children to their bedrooms and then cleaned up the breakfast dishes.

"Where is my coffee?" the voice roared down the hall when the bathroom door opened.

"I put it on the nightstand," Emily answered. "Good morning."

"Humph!" heavy footsteps landed on the hardwood floors towards the bedroom. Then with the coffee cup in hand, Jack went into the living room.

After washing the dishes and starting a load of laundry, Emily checked on her husband. She hoped that the morning coffee soothed the gruffness out of him. When Emily entered the living room, she could see Jack reading the newspaper.

"Do you need more coffee?" Emily asked.

"Maybe a topper," responded the grumpy man.

Emily picked up the cup and carried it to the kitchen. She poured more of the black liquid into the cup. Then returned the cup to its spot in the living room. Emily then headed into the bedroom to make the bed and tidy up in there.

"How is Ruth?"

The question caused Emily to pause and look up from the bed. "Feeling better," she replied.

"Did George return from maneuvers?" Jack asked, knowing that Ruth's husband regularly attended military training drills.

"Next week he comes back, I think." Emily answered. After eight years, the couple's conversation had become superficial.

In the afternoon, Jack asked Emily to go for a cat tide with him. He said that they needed to talk privately. Emily checked on the children and explained that they would be right back. Then Jack and Emily left the house. Jack unlocked the car doors and positioned himself in the driver's seat. Emily got into the passenger seat, curious about where they were going.

Jack headed the vehicle to the gas station, where he stopped to fill the tank and then purchased cigarettes and beer. When Jack returned to the car, he headed the car down the highway.

"Where are we going?" Emily asked, trying to sound casual.

"You will see." Jack glanced in her direction and flashed his salesman's smile.

The car made its way down the highway in wordless silence. At the stoplight, Jack turned the car southwards. They silently rode until Jack turned onto a gravel road.

Jack opened his mouth as his foot pushed in the accelerator. "You need to keep those bratty kids' mouths shut in the morning so I can sleep. I work hard all week long; weekends, I need sleep to rest up for the coming week." Jack scolded Emily as the car sped down the gravel road.

"Sorry, I know you like to sleep late, but the kids could not go outside to play." Emily apologized.

"They should have gotten sent back to bed," Jack continued.

"Next time." Emily softly answered. The car's speed made Emily fearful. This fast on a gravel road without slowing for curves seemed irrational to her. As they rounded another bend, Emily held onto her armrest. She scanned her husband's face and began to open her mouth to complain.

"Where did you go this morning?" Jack asked.

"I told you. Ruth's and then the grocery store."

"Did you see him?"

"Who?" Emily asked as she looked at her husband with curiosity and confusion.

"Your boyfriend!"

"What?" Emily replied, shocked at the answer from Jack.

The car sped up. Emily saw the sharp curve ahead. She grasped the armrest firmly and placed her free hand on the dashboard. A brief loud pop from the rear of the car occurred before the vehicle fishtailed into a yard. Emily felt relief that the car stopped.

Jack got out of the car and walked around to examine what happened. "The tire came off the rim. You sit here while I put the wheel back together." Jack told Emily. "Then you will tell me about your boyfriend."

Something about Jack's voice and actions worried Emily. A feeling of doom flooded her limbs with adrenaline. She watched as Jack walked to the nearest house. When Emily could not see Jack, she placed her hand on the car door and released the catch to slip out of the car. Emily left the car door open and fled down the gravel road. She prayed that she could get home to the children before Jack fixed the vehicle. Emily continued to run down the gravel road. Refusing to slow her pace, Emily finally needed to catch her breath.

When her breathing steadied, Emily resumed traveling down the road. She switched between a jog and a brisk walk, trying to cover distance quickly. Occasionally, Emily glanced back over her shoulder. Emily still held on to the belief that she could make it home before Jack. When Emily saw a cloud of dust rising from the road behind her, she knew Jack had fixed the tire.

And he would be coming after her. She began racing down the road, trying to maintain the lead.

She could hear the car's approach. Panic rose in Emily's chest as adrenaline pumped her legs faster. She started scanning the ditch and fields as her brain hurriedly pieced together a plan. Emily spied a road grader sitting on the side of the road. The sound of the car grew louder, the dust cloud behind the car grew thicker. Emily knew she had to get out of sight before the car appeared around the curve. She sprinted towards the heavy road machine and crouched down next to the large dual tires. She prayed that she would not get discovered.

Emily carefully listened to the engine, monitoring the car's movement as the sound increased with every rotation of the tires across the gravel. The woman forced herself to stay hidden, resisting the urge to peek out. She inhaled deeply and held her breath, listening to the flinging of gravel with the car's speedy approach. Even from her hiding spot, Emily could see the dense dust cloud as she released her breath.

The engine roared, closing in on her position. She held her breath again as the dust cloud enveloped her. The roar traveled arouse on her right side, continued to pass the machine, and disappeared on her left side. Emily momentarily felt relieved that her hiding spot went undetected. The feeling got quickly replaced by discouragement at failing to escape. Emily headed home, praying that her children were safe and feeling that the situation grew direr with each passing minute.

Dejection from the failure prodded her return to the house. Emily noticed Jack's car did not sit in front of the house. He thought that his continued search for her sparked a bit of hope. Then the quietness of the place slapped Emily in the face. She knew that Jack had taken her children.

In the previous story, we saw a woman's failed escape from her blight. She tried to take advantage of an unexpected opportunity. But for a successful flight to freedom, a person needs to prepare for their life afterward. Their escape requires planning and timing in addition to opportunity.

This preparation may sound harsh and challenging, but it becomes necessary to protect oneself in a fight for your life. There are some things that the person will need to have available to establish a new residency. And if children get involved, then even more items need inclusion.

· Driver's License
· Social security card
· Passport (if owned)

- Cash
- Birth certificate
- Copy of marriage license
- Copy of lease agreement or mortgage agreement
- Title to the car if they are the sole owner
- Individual accounts for credit cards, cell phones, and banking. If both names get listed on an account, then leave those documents behind.

A person may believe that their abuser does not care or pay attention. This belief is farthest from the truth. Abusers tend to be aware of details that the world would take for granted. So, to leave with the above documents, subterfuge becomes necessary. A cunning strategy involves a friend holding these documents for when you are out of the home.

Often a gaslighter will attempt to regain the control they had over the victim. A person should prepare a strong defense as a response to any possible actions of the gaslighter. The strong defense should establish the individual's ownership of feelings, ideas, and opinions and the responsibility boundary for these expressions. Here are some examples of responses to commonly used gaslighting phrases:

- A gaslighter accuses its victim of being too sensitive. An appropriate response could be, "My

feelings are neither right nor wrong, and I am entitled to them."
- A gaslighter accuses its victim of being crazy. A calm and appropriate response could be, "I will not continue this discussion until you can talk respectfully with me." Then walk away without saying another word.
- A gaslighter accuses its victim of making things up. A calm and appropriate response could be, "We have two different viewpoints on the subject, and I am permitted to express my opinion."
- When a gaslighter accuses their victim of over-reacting, an appropriate response could be, "Please do not minimize my feelings when I discuss things with you."

A week after the failed flight to freedom, Emily walked in the door after work. Jack met her in the kitchen. He grabbed the collar of her coveralls and lifted her feet off the floor. "Where have you been?" he screamed in her face.

Emily managed to cough at "work' in the middle of her coughs from choking.

Jack tossed Emily onto the floor. "You got off work five hours ago. Where have you been?" The toe of Jack's shoe landed under Emily's ribs. Jack walked around the body kicking at Emily every couple of steps.

Emily managed to curl into the fetal position on the floor. Her hands covered the back of her neck, and her knees got drawn to protect her abdomen. She knew the kicks were landing on her face, and she tried to hide her face with her elbows. "The entire plant had to stay and work late. And mandatory overtime this Saturday." Emily repeatedly cried out, "I tried to call home to let you know, but no one answered."

"Mommy? Daddy?" Emily heard coming from the kitchen doorway. And then footsteps running to a bedroom, and bed springs squeaking as the child got back into bed.

Jack finally walked into the other room, leaving Emily curled up on the floor. She listened with dread, wondering if Jack would spank the child. The man's footsteps told Emily that her husband headed towards the living room.

Emily carefully rose from the floor. Exhaustion from the long hours at work and hurting all over from the kicking, Emily leaned on the kitchen sink for a few minutes. Then she heard her husband's footsteps coming towards the kitchen. She turned around as he stomped towards her from the doorway.

"So. what time did you get off?" the man asked.
"Around 5 o'clock." She replied.
"And you came straight home?"

"Yes, a couple of friends wanted to go for coffee, but I told them no."

Emily watched as Jack's face turned red with rage. He began throwing anything within arm's reach at Emily. Emily's thoughts whirled with confusion. She sidestepped a fishing pole flying towards her. The clattering of the fishing pole distracts her from trying to plan an escape. Fear shot through her as Jack took two steps towards her. Emily picked up the fishing pole, flung it in Jack's general direction before dashing out the door.

Emily raced to her car and drove off. She felt a sense of urgency, so she drove around the block. Emily considered her options at the corner. She felt if she re-entered the house that Jack would kill her. She decided to get a cup of coffee so she could calm down and think.

As Emily pulled into the restaurant's parking lot, she recognized the cars of some friends. She relaxed a little with the knowledge that some people cared. Emily walked into the restaurant and joined the table where her friends sat.

"Hi," Emily greeted them, trying to maintain a calm exterior to hide her inner turmoil.

"Umm, hi," Rebecca said as she quickly elbowed her husband, Leroy.

"Hey, how you been girly?" Leroy said, quickly averting his eyes.

"Long time no ..." Jason cut his words short as he

scanned Emily's face. "What happened? Did you have an accident?"

Emily felt her tears forming as she replied, "No." She turned her coffee cup over so the waitress and moved it to the edge of the table could fill it.

"Are you alright?"

"I think so." Emily answered.

"Here, drink this,' Rebecca said, pushing the coffee towards Emily.

The conversation focused on the night's work. The employees appreciated the overtime but complained about the lack of notice. Then they talked about the upcoming festival and jugging to catch fish. Emily relaxed with the warmth of the coffee and conversation.

"Guys, we need to head out. The kids will get up soon." Leroy explained as he and Rebecca got up from the table. "Jason, are you coming?"

"No, I want to make sure that Emily will be alright. Sarah stayed with her folks so I have time."

Emily looked at her coffee as another swell of tears threatened her eyes.

"Okay, see you later dude." Leroy said before walking off.

Jason looked at Emily. Her face turning purple with bruising, and the woman's nearly half swollen eyes gazed past his ear. "Now, tell me what happened. Did your husband do this?" He had already guessed at what happened and wanted to determine his friend's frame of mind.

"Yes. When I walked in the door ..." Emily proceeded to explain everything to her friend. When she finished, Emily felt some tears roll down her cheeks.

Emily and Jason discussed Emily's options for the next hour. They finally developed a plan to get Emily's children without risking Emily's safety. Emily knew that she could use her uncle's summer house in an emergency. Jason picked up Emily's children at the agreed location and then drove them to their mom.

When Emily saw Jason's car returning, she sighed with relief. The car parked in the closest spot as the children hopped out to meet their mom. Emily wrapped her arms around her four children and kissed each one on the forehead. She then put her children in the car before turning to thank Jason.

"Sarah will wonder where I am, so I need to head home." Jason explained.

"Thank you."

"Are you sure you have a place to stay?"

"Yes. We will be fine. Thank you again." A smile of relief appeared in Emily's eyes.

When Emily left the parking lot, she went directly to Ruth's. Emily felt grateful that she had the foresight to leave some emergency belongings with her friend. But unease would accompany Emily until they left the area.

When Ruth opened her front door, she did not recognize Emily at first.

"Hi. I came for that box of stuff." Emily said.

"What box? Who are you?" Ruth asked before recognizing Emily. "Oh my god. Are you alright? Why did he do this to you?"

Emily explained what happened when she arrived home from work. Then she told Ruth her plan to go to her uncle's. "I will call to let you know when we arrive." Emily told Ruth before getting into the car.

The police knocked on the door to do a wellness check the following day. He explained that he wanted to make sure they were alright. Emily's eyes began to water, and she felt that her facial appearance required explaining. So, she told the officer what had happened and why they had taken refuge in her uncle's house. The officer jotted down Emily's answers to his questions before leaving the peninsula.

Emily and her children had a quiet day of rest. Emily called her uncle. She explained what occurred and asked his permission to stay. Then she took the children to the grocery store to buy food. The remainder of the day Emily spent with the children.

While Emily made breakfast the following day, she saw her husband's car approaching the house. Emily herded her children into a bedroom and called the police. She embraced them and whispered, "We need to stay quiet as a mouse right now."

They heard a knock on the door. Emily put a finger to her lips, signaling the children to stay quiet. Jack let the screen door slam shut when he walked around the house. Then there came a knock on the back door. Emily signaled quietly once more as she went to the window to peek outside.

Emily watched the squad car approach to where her husband's car sat. Two offices got out and examined the vehicle. Emily saw her husband talk to the officers, and then one officer walked up the sidewalk to the house. Emily told her kids to stay in the bedroom while she spoke to the policeman.

Emily opened the door when the officer knocked. She quickly latched the screen door as she greeted the officer. Emily felt fearful that her husband would lunge at her to get into the house.

"Are you and the children safe?"

"Yes sir." Emily answered.

"Have you talked with your uncle?" The officer continued.

"Yes sir."

"We followed up with the caretaker for the house yesterday. They said that you can stay." The officer informed Emily.

"Thank you."

"We will escort your husband off the property. He

just wanted to know that you brought the children here." The officer added.

"I see. As you can see, we are fine." Emily replied.

"We will add an extra patrol of this neighborhood. Although I do not think your husband will bother you anymore."

"Okay, thank you, sir.' Emily said before closing the door.

The next day, Emily's supervisor told her security had escorted Emily's husband from the premises. He had tried to enter the building to see Emily forcefully. And that the police received notification from upper management. Emily realized that her well-being depended on security measures. This tale demonstrates the extent that an abuser goes to re-establish control.

However, once away from their tormentor, a person might display onset signs of trauma. Television shows and movies have shaped our perceptions of trauma and mental health. But typically, they portray the extreme forms that affect the public. Psychological thrillers tend to reflect the murderous intentions, not the aftermath of the plans. The intent aftermath houses trauma both physical and emotional. Generally, the initial and immediate trauma reactions can be a shock-like physical exhibition:

· Confusion

- Exhaustion
- Agitation
- Anxiety
- Numbness
- Dissociation

Some indicators of delayed trauma responses can include:

- Sleep disorders
- Nightmares
- Flashbacks
- Avoidance of any association with the event
- Recurrence dread
- Hypervigilance

People can recover from traumatic events; however, intervention can dramatically improve recovery. Rarely do these aftermath indicators and recovery periods get presented on a screen. Uninvolved people rarely understand the destructive nature of gaslighting effects on a victim. The individual disappears into a shell state as a necessary component to cope and recover from the stress of enduring gaslighting. Most people will expect the victim to walk away free. Outsiders believe that anger and hurt will sever any emotional ties to the abuser. However, this rarely occurs for victims that have endured abuse.

Any abuse can cause a person to ask the question, "Why me?" But prolonged exposure to abuse damages more than the notion of "wrong place at the wrong time." The recesses of the psyche where an individual hosts their self-esteem, beliefs, hopes, and dreams become blocked off. Meanwhile, the person's emotions and feelings become hidden from view propelling the person's actions can become irrational and out of place. This break in the psyche needs the attention and guidance that mental health therapists provide.

Without the necessary attention and understanding, a person loses hope. They feel forced into the dire position of giving up their survival to find relief and peace. Often attempted suicide becomes a person's loud cry asking for help coping with a difficult situation. However, some victims feeling extremely discouraged, become so desperate for relief that they see the only option as suicide. This tragic ending might be brutal for most people to comprehend unless they have traveled along the same path towards utter despair.

A familiar feeling that a victim carries with them and needs to overcome can be worthlessness. The abuser demonstrated little regard or respect for their victim and established that the victim had no value. The victim felt worthless and accepted the feeling as a fact. Essentially, their worthlessness caused an identity crisis. An internal conflict between the perceived points and the person's self-awareness takes place. The battle can become noticeable when the person exhibits confusion and indecisiveness. The feeling of shame enters the conflict. It then acts as an amplifier echoing all the doubts and misconceptions carried by the words "why me" and "if I."

The burden of feelings and thoughts that a victim carries can be exhausting. Often, weakened by the internal turmoil that victim feels weariness throughout their body. There comes a desire to wrap oneself in a cottony cocoon that provides sensory deprivation. Sleep cannot replenish the energy lost by an individual's essence to this fatigue. Reflection and rebirth over time will ease the core's fatigue.

However, we will need to learn to forgive ourselves at the same time. Forgiveness does not imply that we accept responsibility for the abuser's actions. This forgiveness for "ourselves" stems from a place of loving devotion and sacrifice. The compassion that each of us feels often forces a person into sacrificing their well-being for the well-being of someone else. While this deed can be considered noble, we sometimes need to temper our actions with tough love. We need to allow the other guy in a situation to face the consequences for what they do.

As compassionate individuals, our focus needs to be on the influence our actions possess on another's future and not always the present situation. Most people want to seem kind, loving, and supportive. Often our parents taught us to behave this way in society. Although one fact often gets overlooked – each of us deserves the same treatment. After all, as a single entity of the world, we simultaneously get affected by the effects of our actions. Rarely is the practice of tough love learned before adulthood. And once an adult, people tend to believe that they cannot know anything else about living.

After earnestly forgiving ourselves, we need acceptance for our quirks. Tough love wrote the previous statement. These two actions will begin the process of emotional recovery more than anything else will. These actions are our key to open the door to willingness.

Chapter 6

Chapter 6: Walking in the Sun Again

Chapter 6: Walking in the Sun Again

A victim suffered for the most extended time as the abuser whittle away at personal space and morale. These aspects may not be as resilient and self-healing as the body's tissues. The victim became ingrained with the negative thinking that the abuser used to break through the morale and invade the space. Think of the abuser as a termite that has chewed away at a person's foundations. And what is the best way to get rid of termites? Professional exterminators need summoning.

And in this situation, the professional exterminators are therapists and counselors. After undergoing the harrowing experience of gaslighting abuse, only the shell of a person exists. The individual's psyche seems drained of strength and energy. The person needs to recover their essence, revive their resolve, and reorganize their perceptions for living. There exist many ways to accomplish these objectives, and we will examine a few of them.

Sage individuals become educated in helping people recover their spirit. These individuals can offer a variety of tools as well as act as a sounding board. As a sounding board, therapists and counselors listen to what an individual says. Then they help the individual acknowledge and identify different feelings. Often therapists and counselors work in conjunction with a psychiatrist or psychologist. The educational background distinguishes the differing title given to these professionals. Generally, psychiatrists get licensed to prescribe medications. A few states in the United States permit psychologists to prescribe medications. Therapists and counselors can refer a person to a psychiatrist for further evaluation or treatments more advanced than simple therapies.

A psychiatrist possesses a medical degree, a specialty in psychiatry and may acquire advanced skills from a residency. Typically, psychiatrists treat individuals that require medication as part of the treatment plan. A psychiatrist will base a diagnosis on the results of psychological testing, physical examinations, laboratory tests, and one on one evaluations.

After collecting all the assessment data for an individual, the psychiatrist will determine the best treatment plan. Often, acute cases will get referred for psychotherapy and short-term medication intervention. And more severe cases may require the intervention of medical procedures to assist in the recovery.

One such mechanical therapy, light therapy, uses artificial light to simulate sunlight for individuals that suffer from seasonal depression. Typically, the patient will sit near a lightbox for about 10 to 15 minutes. The box will emit between 2,500 and 10,000 lux. The more powerful the lightbox, the shorter the treatment time. Often, new patients will get prescribed a more temporary dose of light until their body gets acclimated.

Psychotherapy, also called talk therapy, can be outlined in various styles and approaches. Commonly used treatments are:

- Cognitive behavior therapy helps someone understand and change how thoughts and behaviors affect how they feel and act.
- In interpersonal therapy, individuals learn new ways to express feelings or communicate positively. Each individual learns to understand and alter how they address issues and develop tools and methods of management.
- Psychodynamic therapy deals with past experiences and how those experiences affect an indi-

vidual's present thoughts and behaviors. Often, people are unaware of these influences. Once sources for emotional disturbances get identified, therapy can help the individual regain control of their life by addressing the issues.

· Family therapy and relationship therapy provide a safe arena for intimate relations to discuss viewpoints, understand each other, explore feelings, find solutions, and strengthen relationships. Often, patients require an improvement in the cohesion of their support system.

· Typically, group therapy involves 5 to 15 patients with similar problems meeting with a therapist. Typically, group therapy meets once or twice a week and lasts for one to four hours. The therapist encourages everyone to participate in the discussions. This form of treatment can assist a patient in knowing that they are not alone.

Psychotherapy can be highly effective when a person desires recovery. However, recovery may take some time, depending on the severity of personal disruption and willingness to participate. Often, addicts are told not to expect overnight recovery from a condition that took years to develop. This same advice can apply to recovery from emotional and mental abuse. Think of each of the inflicted injuries caused by an abuser as an avocado. A hardened skin encases the soft flesh of emotions and feelings surrounding the pit of pain. Removing a seed from an avocado requires the avocado to get opened. The victim's feelings need expressing before an individual can release their pain pit.

Other forms of psychotherapy incorporate tasks, toys, or animals. Artists, composers, musicians, and writers tap into their creative fountain of emotions and feelings to help them express themselves. This source exists in everyone, although all may not tap into it. But when individuals write in a journal or diary or doodle a flower on a piece of paper, they wet their desire for expression.

Many individuals journal to track their daily events or dreams or keep diaries to record their dates and romantic fantasies. A person does not need to participate in therapy to receive beneficial stress relief or hope from writing in a journal or diary. Sometimes a person does not know how to start writing, often referred to as writer's block. The simplest way to overcome this little fear of putting words on paper requires a person to put letters on paper. While this exhibits general semantics, this method works.

If a person requires the structure of a form to complete, then the following suggestion will be beneficial. Every new entry in a journal or diary should begin on a new page. Before writing any thoughts, opinions, ideas, hopes, or dreams, write out the day and date on the top line. The second line describes the weather conditions for the day. On the third line, identify your emotions, such as sad, happy, upset, crying, joyful, etc. You are ready to begin writing, so write T – h. Generally, journal sentences will start with either "The" or "There." Some entries will begin with "I"; however, beginners to journaling usually do not feel intimate with the process in the beginning. Do not read while you write. Journaling and diaries should not receive editing. They record a person's thoughts in the moment, not as an after-thought. If you notice a connection between stress and addictive behavior, such as smoking or overeating, identifying this con-nection would be appropriate for the journal. You may even want to assign a line for "How many ___" ciga-rettes, drinks, or candy bars you had that day. Add these lines up and keep track of your progress at the end of a week or month. As a person grows more con-fident and learns to trust their judgment, there will be a correlation with a decrease in the numbers.

Some people may not know how to express what they envision in their mind's eye. Often, our night-mares and dreams will reveal our terrors, fears, desires, and hopes. A way of expressing these can be achieved through pictures. There are numerous ways to create an image.

Some people enjoy the involvement of sketching,

drawing, and painting. Creative fulfillment exists in watching an image appear from the movement of a pencil over a sheet of paper. Or a satisfaction felt when colors are captured on a palette and then transferred to canvas allowing a paintbrush to reveal an unseen image. Other people capture images on film, whether they capture the pleading sadness of a child's eyes when hungry or the exhilaration felt when winning a race.

However, not everyone can go to a location to shoot film, so they scour magazines and newspapers for images that will fit together to form a picture. Some people recycle wood and metal to release the soul in these items, thereby expressing their mind's eye. And others extract shapes and creatures from functional materials, such as clay and paper. As we can see, there are many forms of creative expression, and the method to accomplish these expressions follows the same path.

· Envision a form
· Determine how to recreate that form
· Gather the necessary materials or equipment
· Use feelings and emotions to guide your fingers
· Do not second-guess your work; you are creating an expression from you
· When you finish, turn around and walk away.

A person may feel exhausted after the process, and this means that catharsis has been achieved. When the burden of pent-up emotions and feelings gets released from a person, usually that person feels prepared to sleep. Frequently, an indescribable weariness accompanies catharsis, a sense of relief rushes through the body, and muscles sapped of their strength as shoulders sag and arms fall limp. A warm liquid may flood the lower eyelid, released to rinse away the tears of sadness. And when the person observes their creation, the sense that hurt no longer haunts them as joy fills an empty spot in their soul.

In Chapter 4, we presented phrases that a person may hear from an abuser. These phrases were words of destruction. However, these exact words can be a starting point to rebuild a person's shattered psyche. We can create affirmations and mantras to counter the echoes of these destructive phrases. Consider the following:

- Stop being so sensitive.
- You are too soft-hearted!
- You are too emotional about this! You are just overly sensitive.

If we turn the above into, "thank you for acknowledging my uniqueness."

- You are crazy.
- You are just paranoid.
- Stop being crazy!
- You have an active imagination.

We can turn the above into, "I am insightful and can trust my thoughts."

- It is not a big deal.
- I do not know why you are making such a big deal about this!
- You are overreacting.
- Cut the drama!
- I was joking!
- I was kidding!
- You have no sense of humor.
- You are making that up.
- Do not get so worked up.
- You are blowing everything out of proportion!

And we can turn these rantings into, "I define my life."

- That never happened.

- We never went there.
- We never did that.
- You never remember things clearly.
- Pattern? There is no pattern.
- There you go again, diving into the deep end.
- You see something that is not there.
- Stop being hysterical!
- You are hysterical.

Then we can practice, "I am free of the negative restraints."

- You make me laugh.
- We will not want to go through this again!
- You are trying to confuse me.
- There you go again; you are so ungrateful.
- You are wrong, and you never remember things.
- Stop lying!
- Where did you get such a crazy idea?
- It is all in your head.

We can counter the above with "Thank you for giving me the courage to live."

- You are insecure.
- Stop being so insecure.

- I cannot handle your insecurity!
- Messing up is the reason why I cannot trust you!
- Forgetting is the reason why I do not put faith in you!
- I do not understand what you are saying.
- You are making stuff up, as usual.
- Why should I believe you? No one else does.
- Nobody believes a word you say; why should I?
- Oh, come on, I would never say anything like that.
- Oh, come on, I never said that!

A counter for the above turns the phrases into "I am a rational being in control of life."

These simple affirmations create a perfect way to welcome each new day. And they can establish new beliefs to counter intrusive and destructive memories of a past life. After someone escapes from an abuser, the conditioning from the repeated attacks remains with the person as baggage. We need to leave this baggage at the claims window, and the only way a person can do that – actively control one's thought patterns. Daily affirmations present a way to establish that control and achieve a person's dreams.

Mantras are beneficial for meditating. Once a person begins to feel like a human instead of a caged animal, they can diverge from affirmations to mantras of harmony. The sound of a mantra allows the mind and soul to meet at a focal point. This union strengthens a person's self-awareness and perceptions of life. As a mantra hums in harmony with the world, a person can feel the stress draining away with their exhalations and peace entering with every inhalation.

Meditating allows a person to calm the energies, worries, and frets that often plague people and create an abode of tranquility for the mind. As a person fixates on a focal point and allows nature's energies to penetrate vacated areas, the whirlpool of stress gets pushed into the focal point. The person's body will naturally relax with the release of the daily tension. A tingling may surge up through the spine as grounded energy pulsates into them, massaging their soul from the inside out.

The grounding established by meditation will help strengthen a person's convictions when they repeat the daily affirmations. The soul's fortifications built on the duality of affirmations and meditations provides the essence of individual security. A person's sense of security releases all self-doubts, fears, and vigilance, permitting recovery from personal terrors. Soon the person's breathing eases with deepening breaths, and silently the air flows in and out until the people no longer hear the blood rushing through their veins. The world around them seems calmer and life's pace slower.

Often serene environments envisioned during

meditation can develop into self-hypnosis. The prin-
ciples of mind over matter can produce relaxation
and stress reduction. Recalling specific positive affirmations and mantras can trigger this relaxation or
boost a person's self-image. Typically, therapists will
instruct individuals suffering from anxiety in the
method of self-hypnosis. Although the yogic practice
of progressive muscle relaxation closely mirrors self-
hypnosis.

Some forms of meditation can also get considered
as exercises, such as yoga and tai chi. Movement
causes endorphins to be released, and these feel-good
hormones can help in the recovery from abuse. The
Hindu practice of yoga can be considered a meditation or exercise form. Yet, the philosophy behind yoga
extends into the vastness of the universe. The term
yoga means "union," however, yoga can be interpreted
as "that which leads to reality." The central focus on
respiration and controlled breathing while maintain-
ing reflective energy poses stimulates new pathways
for awareness. These new insights into a person's inner consciousness can illuminate weaknesses or
faults in one's beliefs and ideas, thus reconstructing
alternatives to the old ways.

The Chinese martial art practice of tai chi directs a
person to box a person's shadow skillfully. This mov-
ing meditation form focuses on controlled graceful-
ness with deliberate leisure taken to achieve flowing

movements. These movements, along with regulated breathing, improve a person's circulation of oxygen supply to the body's cells and renew vital energies. This fresh supply of oxygen can alleviate stress and improve mood. Frequently, instructors will begin each class by instructing students to draw the earth's energy up through their legs before leading them through the 108 movements.

Often, the more aggressive forms of exercise, such as running or kickboxing, can sweat a person's hostilities out while tiring an individual into relaxing their defenses. In this manner, the body strengthens itself while endorphins promote a healthy outlook. Any aerobic exercise will release stale air with a fresh supply of oxygenated air. The body critically needs oxygen to produce energy. Healthy supplies of oxygen carried by red blood cells through the body's tributaries can counter the effects of cortisol.

Cortisol can get thought of as the body's fire alarm. The human body produces this steroid-based hormone in response to stress, both actual and imagined. Cortisol releases glucose necessary for the brain and cell growth to function correctly. Cortisol prepares the body for endurance during stress. In contrast, adrenaline prepares a person to fight or flee a perceived threat. Excessive cortisol in the body from prolonged stress can affect a person and cause:

- Elevated blood pressure
- Osteoporosis
- Libido cessation
- Easily bruised
- Dry mouth
- Muscle weakness
- Swift increase in weight
- Mood swings
- Incessant urination

Meanwhile, prolonged stress and excessive stress hormones adversely affect the body by impacting blood flow. Symptoms of this include:

Broken-heart syndrome, a condition that occurs when the blood flow gets reduced due to extreme emotional distress

- Dizziness
- Light-headedness
- Irritability
- Panic attacks
- Anxiety
- Trouble sleeping
- Nervousness

If a person can identify with any of the above symptoms, they should speak with their physician or psychiatrist. These symptoms may be an indicator of a medication treatment plan for both physical and mental health. Medical practitioners should get consulted about exercise and alternative medicines or treatments before these lifestyle additions.

Although walking does not require a physician's consent, our daily walking action provides a means of easy exercise. However, the body knows the difference between walking for exercise and cleaning the house, shop, or work. When you decide to walk for exercise, a good idea starts with leaving your home to do. It would be best if you prepared for the walk by wearing a watch, taking a cell phone, and bringing some water. Some people use a pedometer to track the number of steps they take to meet daily fitness goals. Shopping malls and walking paths often post distances accomplished when someone walks a specific route.

You can benefit from keeping a written record of your walks. When you review the documents, you can see your improvement if the distance lengthens for the same length or the time shortens for the same stretch walked. This improvement denotes the increase in your endurance for your physical well-being.

When beginning your walking for exercise, a person should start with a short distance that does not affect their breathing. For instance, a walk of 15 – 30 minutes will suffice for most sedentary beginners, more active beginners can easily do 40 – 60 minutes. Please remember that you will need to turn around to get back if you walk in a straight line. So, 30 minutes in a straight line will end up being 60 minutes or more of walking. If you find that your muscles are achy from walking, then rest the next day so the muscles can heal. Endurance gets developed by steady improvements for a task.

Chapter 7

Chapter 7: Path to Renewal

Chapter 7: Path to Renewal

Forewarned: the following pages contain help and hope, but you will need to participate in the creation. As a victim, this cannot get easily accomplished due to its intense nature. For survivors, this participation becomes slightly more manageable.

However, since you read this far, our confidence lies with you.

We understand the problems and issues that arise after escaping ongoing abuse. And how a person's moods and emotions fluctuate. Initially, there occurs a honeymoon period of exhilaration for our freedom. Then a person progresses into a need for direction and structure.

That direction can be discovered in the following pages.

However, lingering ghosts of what took place, uncertainty about the future, and distrust in our decisions will arise. Often people need to battle the demons from their past. People can find the best method for doing this in the mnemonic word DEMONS:

- Doze
- Exercise
- Meditation
- Outside
- Nourishment
- Sociable

The human body requires rest for self-healing and rejuvenation. Dozing, naps, and sleep will provide the body with the necessary rest. During periods of rest, the body uses energy to repair and make new cells. When active, the body uses energy for the movement of the person's appendages.

The exercise process allows the muscles to stay in condition to perform the necessary pumping action required by the circulation system. Since the body depends on this pumping action to move beneficial chemicals to needed spots and remove toxins from the body, the muscles demand conditioning and strengthening.

Frequently, our thoughts become overcrowded, and we cannot concentrate on a specific idea. Meditation allows our brains to experience a temporary cessation from all transient ideas, images, and thoughts. This solitude for the brain refreshes its connections and firing patterns, thereby permitting more precise focus for the individual.

Even though we live in air-conditioned environments, the human body's constitution demands the vast expanse of being outside in the sunlight. Our lungs relish the movement of fresh air into them and pushing out the residual spent stale air. Meanwhile, the pores in our skin languish with the caressing rays of sunlight, imbuing them with needed nutrients for functioning.

The energy necessary to move our bodies needs replenishing regularly. This nourishment comes from proper nutrition and a routine eating/fasting schedule. Eating determines how nutrients get supplied, while the fasting periods allow processes in the body to deliver nutrients.

Everyone needs some contact with other individuals to maintain a positive outlook. The information received by the brain from seeing, smelling, and sensing other people establishes the togetherness connection. This connection reinforces the difference between loneliness and alone. Without this frequent reminder, our thoughts will gradually determine that no one else exists. Then we grieve for the loss of fellow humans in our life and feel alone in the world.

When we remember the fundamentals necessary to battle our demons, we can experience life. Unfortunately, the fundamentals do not heal the wounds inflicted by abuse. Those wounds require special attention and time to heal. Sometimes our wounds fester from our negative thinking.

As a defense against all the negatives that can affect a person, we ask that a safety plan get made. The safety plan should provide answers to the following questions and place for easy access.

Safety Plan

- What do I need to do to return to positive thinking?
- What warning signs or triggers will make me feel as if I'm speeding downhill without brakes?
- What have I successfully done in the past to improve?
- What ways of coping do I have?
- What should I do to help calm and self-soothe?

- What should I tell myself to counter my dark thoughts?
- What would I say to a friend who felt this way?
- What could others do that would help comfort me?
- Who can I call? (List one or two friends or relatives, one or two health professionals, one or two telephone helplines.)
- Where can I go that provides me safety?

You need to share this Safety Plan with someone trustworthy. Suppose any individual feels suicidal after doing everything on their safety plan. In that case, they need to contact 911 or get to an emergency room.

Throughout our lives, everything around us modernizes with changes. If we do not change along with life, we shrivel up and become bitter from our refusal to change. Frequently, coping skills need to be recognized or developed to handle crises and change. We outlined tasks to accomplish these needs. These suggested tasks can guide a person through a difficult or confusing period of floundering when learning how to become independent.

Coping skills apply to individuals' internal strength to offset or overcome adversities, disadvantages, or disabilities without amending or eliminating underlying conditions. A person might consider these skills as "workarounds" or "tools" Throughout life, we encounter difficulties, opportunities, and challenges that require us to cope. Our failure to do so will prevent our growth and hinder any progression forward.

Our reformation needs to begin with a feeling of comfortability of who we are inside our bodies. And to help with our reformation, we need three things: defining, organizing, and planning. Knowing these things can boost your self-confidence and inspire you to change. We need to identify:

- Three things that you like about yourself
- Three ways that you take care of yourself
- Three areas that you would like to improve
- One way to enhance taking care of yourself

These things, ways, and areas should get posted prominently as a reminder of your self-appreciation. This new boost of self-appreciation will establish the positive mindset required for the following exercises.

Next, we would like for you to write a statement of intent. The message should resemble the following:

- My intent now is to live my life. I am aware that

I have choices in every situation. I will select the paths that contribute to my daily growth and peace.

· Each day I do the best that I am able.
· I will identify my obstacles to happiness.
· I regulate my thoughts and actions.
· I allow myself to chase my dreams.
· I refuse any role or circumstance requiring the surrender of my inclinations.

Now that you have created a pact with yourself, we can begin using tools to help us understand ourselves. Professionals and nonprofessionals have made different diagnostic tests throughout the years, such as "Who is your ideal partner?" Often, these tests get written for people's entertainment.

However, these simple assessments can provide a new perspective about ourselves. So, they can be beneficial in the long run. The following questions can help establish our life purpose.

We will be creating a personal mission statement for our life away from an abuser. But first, we need to reveal our life purpose. Additionally, these questions can prepare a conducive frame of mind to write a personal mission statement. There are no specific answers to these questions. Unless you share the answers, no one else will see them. You need to allow 15 minutes for this questionnaire.

Instructions:

- Get yourself a couple of sheets of blank paper and a pen or pencil.
- Find a spot free from any interruptions.
- Turn off all phones.
- Give yourself 60 seconds to write each answer, so act quickly.
- Be honest.
- No editing.
- Enjoy this connection to self exercise and keep a SMILE on your face while you write.

Questions:

1. What activities can cause you to lose track of time?
2. What are your deepest values? (List six)
3. What favorite things got done in the past? What are they now?
4. What makes you smile? (Events, hobbies, certain people, activities, special projects, etc.)
5. What causes do you strongly believe in? Connect?
6. What do people typically ask for your help?
7. Who inspires you most? (This can be a person,

living or dead; acquainted or unacquainted.) Which qualities in each person inspire you?

8. What makes you feel great about yourself?

9. What are some hardships, challenges, and difficulties that you have survived or are in the process of overcoming? What did you do to survive?

10. Suppose you face the end of your life; what would you regret not accomplishing, becoming, or having in your life?

11. What are your naturally good assets? (Skills, abilities, gifts, etc.)

12. Suppose you could get a message across to a stadium full of people. Who would fill the stadium as your audience? What would you say in the news?

13. If you needed to teach something, what would you teach?

14. You know your passions, values, and talents. (To people, causes, beings, organizations, environment, planet, etc.) how could you use these attributes to make a positive contribution to brighten someone's day?

15. Imagine that you are now 85 years old, rocking in the chair on your front porch, a spring breeze gently caressing against your cheek. You are blissfully content with the beautiful life you led and peacefully satisfied. When you look back at your life, all that you acquired, and the relation-

ships you developed? (List them out.) What matters to you the most?

Next, title a piece of paper "Verbs" and title a second piece "Nouns" You need to transfer the appropriate words from your answers to the designated paper. The two pages of lists reveal the purpose of your life. All the listed verbs relate to what you want to do in your life, and all the nouns represent the people or objects that can help you succeed.

You are now able to write your mission statement. Often, personal mission statements, referred to as a motto, can inspire a person to face life's challenges. And the message will answer the following two questions:

· What is your purpose?
· What is your mission?

If you do not know how to begin to draft the statement, use the following template:
"I will (insert an action) for (insert an audience) by (insert a skill or skills) to (insert the desired result)."

For instance: "I will write a book for women organizing ideas into words and writing copy to encourage, motivate, and preserve their right to a life of free-thinking and pursuit of happiness."

We successfully established our mission statement, so we need to create a plan to fulfill our purpose. The following guide can help a person stay focused.

1. On a piece of paper, write your objective, mission statement, or role. List the things necessary to achieve your goal, mission statement, or function.
    1. Cash flow
    2. Transportation
    3. Knowledge
    4. Equipment
    5. Talent
    6. Supportive assistance

1. Steps to be taken and when each will occur
1.
2.

3.

4.

5.

Set an end date to review your progress

Each time you review your progress, plan on answering these questions again on a new sheet of paper. Refreshing the questions allows you to stay focused on your goals and eases any confusion or doubts that may creep into your thoughts. Congratulating yourself for any progress that has been achieved promotes inspiration and motivation. Set this as a crucial part of each review that you do. You fled a relationship where acknowledgment got withheld, do not treat yourself in the same manner.

At times, everyone finds it challenging to get motivated to do things. This challenge becomes especially true when we get consumed with a poor self-image or doubts about our abilities. It would be best to permit yourself to take a break; after all, schools provide recess, and companies give regularly scheduled coffee breaks. Even though you are focused on personal goals, you still need to relax.

There are occasions when learning something new can inspire and motivate an individual. Maybe a trip to the library can hold the key for you to become motivated. Or perhaps inspiration found by going to a beauty salon to get your hair or nails done. A lot of women believe that a new haircut gives them a new outlook on life. And for some women, the pampering that occurs when they get manicures and pedicures revives their spirit and helps connect to their femininity. These are leisure time activities, but a break implies leisure time.

A way to handle this indecisiveness or confusion gets provided when we closely examine our likes. Often there are so many activities that can be done during leisure time that a person cannot decide what to do. And engaging in these activities contributes to your physical and mental well-being. So, we will track our leisure activities by completing the following exercise. Please list:

- Name an activity done in leisure time that you do to be physically fit
- Name an activity done in leisure time that you do to compete
- Name an activity done in leisure time that you do to relax
- Name an activity done in leisure time that you do to be alone
- Name an activity done in leisure time that you do to socialize
- Name an activity done in leisure time that you as a spectator

- Name an activity done in leisure time that helps you connect spiritually
- Name an activity done in your leisure time that you do to help others
- Name an activity done in leisure time that you do to learn something new
- Name an activity done in leisure time that you do to feel stimulated
- Name an activity done in leisure time that you do to be creative
- Name an activity done in leisure time that you do for accomplishment

The above answers describe the benefits that you achieve when you participate. Now decide the area(s) you would like to focus on for a break from this chapter.

In chapter six, we learned how to make simple affirmations to counter the voice of negativity in our heads. The promises we make now will stem from surviving the raging storm and setting sail on a new course. Five areas will be provided, answer all five questions to create five new affirmations.

- What negative self-image thoughts do I need to change?
- My affirmation for self-worth

- What ideas will help motivate me?
- My affirmation for inspiration
- What do I require to become healthier mentally, emotionally, spiritually, or physically?
- My pledge for the well-being
- In which areas or ways do I need encouragement?
- My promise for inner strength
- What symptoms or self-defeating behaviors do I need to address?
- My pledge for better mental health

These affirmations create the beginning of your survivor's thinking. Survivor thinking does not erase what you went through to get here. Still, survivor thinking allows you to move away from the pain and develop confidence. As a survivor, you can see the meaning behind the question: If you do the same things in the same ways, how can you expect a different outcome? And the answer is not "because I am crazy!"

We need to learn how to "let go" emotionally. The action of letting go does not mean we will need a box of Kleenex. We will examine both sides of letting go, what it is and is not.

Letting go:

- It does not deny; it accepts

- It does not mean to stop caring; it means you acknowledge that you cannot do it for someone else
- It does not chastise and control anyone but allows dreams to become what you can
- Does not enable, it allows for learning from natural consequences
- Does not cut yourself off; it becomes the realization that you cannot control anyone
- Does not try to change or blame someone; it allows you to be the most you can
- Does admit to powerlessness, meaning the outcome does not depend on you
- It does not "care for," it "cares about"
- Does not judge; it allows people to be human
- It does not "fix"; it acts supportive
- It does not step in to arrange outcomes; it will enable others to affect destinies
- Does not nag, scold, argue or fuss at; it means searching for self-shortcomings and correcting them
- It does not protect. It permits someone else to face reality
- It does not adjust everything to your desires; it cherishes each day as it occurs and yourself
- Does not regret the past; it grows and lives for the future
- Does fear less and love more

As we can see, letting go can further our independence from the past. However, sometimes before a person can let go, they need to stop intrusive thoughts. There are four simple steps to control thoughts. First, we will identify the steps, then demonstrate their application.

- Step 1 Identify your negative thought
- Step 2 Dwell on the identified thought
- Step 3 Interrupt the identified thought
- Step 4 Substitute the negative thinking with a positive or assertive thought

Typically writing a list of your negative thoughts can help when it comes to identifying them. Negative thoughts are any ideas that hack away at a person's self-esteem. So, any fears, self-doubts, insecurities, and phobias should get written on a piece of paper. Review the list in front of you and choose the most uncomplicated negative thought to debunk. Write the chosen thought on top and label it as bothersome thought on the second piece of paper.

Now, concerning this idea that bothers you, answer the five following questions:

1. Is this bothersome thought realistic or unrealistic?

2. Is this bothersome thought productive or counterproductive?
3. Is this irritating idea easy or hard to control?
4. How uncomfortable does this annoying thought make me feel?
5. How much does this annoying thought interfere with my life?

Consider your answers carefully; if you decide that you benefit from ridding yourself of this bothersome thought, then move to the next step. You should prepare for the stage by meditating or becoming extremely relaxed. Coffee and alcohol should not get consumed to relax. Both drinks have a stimulating and then depressing effect physically on the body.

After finding uninterrupted relaxation:

1. Bring the bothersome thought to the front.
2. Focus on the idea for several minutes.
3. Pay tribute to the concept by confronting it with the answers that you provided.
4. Move to the next step.

Different methods can be employed to accomplish step three. Such as wearing a rubber band and snapping it against your wrist when the thought creeps in, pinching yourself, or digging your nails into your skin can work also. Another option requires recording yourself saying, "STOP!" Then, hit the play button when the thought appears.

A more aggressive and active thought countering process requires a 3-minute egg timer. Bring the thought to mind and set the timer. Dwell on the idea for 3 minutes; when the time expires, yell "STOP!", snap your fingers, or stand up quickly. Do not engage in any negative thoughts for at least 30 seconds by keeping your mind blank or thinking of positive words.

Entirely stopping a negative thought will require time and patience. But when you immediately substitute a positive for negative thinking, the recurrences of the idea will lessen. Every negative word that gets replaced displays the proactive behavior necessary to recover from being a victim.

Recovery from victimhood does not occur overnight. Victims feel shame at losing their power. Before the shame can get healed, the person needs to develop and strengthen their ability. Some keys to nurturing emotional energy include:

1. Learning to love self
2. Commitment to change process
3. Finding and living a life based on their inner truth

4. Owning their feelings
5. Looking for and developing inner guidance
6. Establishing appropriate boundaries
7. Recognizing and acting on their wants, needs, and values
8. Showing empathy for themselves and others
9. Expressing negative feelings effectively
10. Finding and using a support system
11. Daily discipline and dedication to empowerment processes

Often, people suffer anxiety when changes occur or need to occur or when they cannot identify their feelings. Meanwhile, actions to stave off feelings of anxiety should get taken. The following methods provide practical ways of handling stress.

1. Take one thing at a time
2. Get enough sleep and rest
3. Talk about your concerns
4. Work off stress
5. Balance work and recreation
6. Avoid self-medicating
7. Do something for others
8. Find a new interest
9. Own your feelings
10. Accept what you cannot control
11. Occasionally give in

12. Be conscious of your behavior patterns
13. Make yourself available
14. Turn stress into a positive force
15. Develop group-oriented activities
16. Have a support system

If the anxiety arises from experiencing unrecognized feelings, the appendix contains a list of frequently unidentified feelings people experience.

Chapter 8

Chapter 8: Where to Get Help

Chapter 8: Where to Get Help

Suppose you can identify any of the signs or symptoms of gaslighting presented throughout this book. As we saw throughout the reading, gaslighting will adversely and significantly affect your mental health, self-esteem, and physical health. In that case, it is critical to seek professional help.

The National Domestic Violence Hotline answers phone calls 24 hours every day of the week and all year long. Their number is 1 (800) 799-SAFE (7233), or TTY, (800) 787-3224, or videophone (for deaf only callers), (206) 518—9361, or the website at thehotline.org to chat with an advocate.

Additionally, you can find help through loveisrespect.org by phoning (866) 331-9474 or texting LOVE IS to 22522.

Or there is a list of resources for help through the National Coalition Against Domestic Violence (NCADV) at ncadv.org/resources.

A doctor can recommend a counselor.

Often a pharmacist has public service information.

A clergy usually has public service information and can offer some abuse counseling.

Local social service agencies, health departments, and police departments will have the contact information for shelters.

Red Cross, Salvation Army, Catholic Charities can also provide information if not crisis intervention.

The law requires most public service agencies to report incidents of suspected abuse. Since various types of abuse get reported to local authorities, cooperate with these individuals. Their job focuses on your safety and well-being. They will intervene on your behalf to protect you. These individuals appreciate and depend on your honesty to properly perform their duties.

Chapter 9

Conclusion

Conclusion

The best advice for living: if you are in any situation where you feel endangered in your life, get out and get help. The topic of this book reveals the serious nature of psychological abuse. The book looks at the people who need to control others and how far they will take it. Recovery from this type of abuse can happen when an individual works towards it. Unfortunately, we cannot force anyone to surrender their pain. Typically, the children carry the horrors with them throughout their lives.

The encounter examples and conversations were based on events experienced and known to occur. These illustrations demonstrated the effects of abuse. Over the years of freedom, our survivors rebuilt their lives. They have not forgotten what they went through, but they healed the injuries. They gained valuable insight into the meaning of living.

Survival makes living possible.

The vivid descriptions found in chapter one provides an understanding of this form of abuse. And the likely results when people tolerate it. Any abuse gets regarded as severe, but psychological abuse occurs slowly. And it reshapes the victim in unseen ways. So, an introduction to trauma was presented concerning the aftermath of gaslighting.

Chapter two gave enlightenment to gaslighting processes and characteristics. Remembering these traits can help a person determine if they hold a victim role. While the situations illustrating random gaslighting differ, the effect of eating away someone's trust and happiness stays the same. Commonly used attributes assist in identifying someone using gaslighting. And some commonly experienced responses to situations. Both the features and reactions can help recognize gaslighting or abuse. However, recognizing and acknowledging are different steps.

An overview of traditional personalities known to implement gaslighting for manipulation of people gets presented in chapter three. A look at some personality disorders and common traits that draw the attention of these predators gets discussed also.

Next, in chapter four, our awareness opens as we

subtly examine tactics and techniques that gaslighters gain power from their victims. As the gaslighter's methods become increasingly more aggressive and demanding, their victim's blight becomes more precarious.

Eventually, the victim falls entirely under the gaslighter's control.

The preparation for escaping from an abuser provided in chapter five can assist in fleeing an abusive situation. The same steps and practices apply. However, gathering the courage and strength to leave the victim needs to muster. Dedication and diligence rest in the hands of the victim for their flight.

The aftermath of prolonged exposure and the forms of help available get discussed in chapter six. The differences between the different professional titles and therapies provide people with an understanding of the type of assistance they want, need, and get. Often people discover that the self-admission that their trust got misplaced comes more difficult than asking for professional help.

In chapter seven, we present a self-help guide for those that want to recover from their harrowing experience. The guide may seem simple enough. But for a person needing help and wanting recovery from the despair and negative feelings progresses through the manual, they will wish for an encouraging anchor.

Chapter eight provides several resources for victims to gain help. Every state and county should offer assistance for victims with a bit of research. Battered women shelters do not readily give out phone numbers or addresses to ensure the safety of their guests.

The appendix lists a variety of feelings and emotions that people go through. Sometimes identifying a feeling or emotion becomes problematic when a person suffers anxieties or fears. The list groups these feelings and emotions by the impact on a person's self-esteem.

The world is not as shocking and horrific a place as this book makes it appear. And not everyone is so worried about self-gratification that they will disregard their fellow man. We must dare to live life to the fullest and find backing from all around us. Support does not shift responsibility from our shoulders; it braces and strengthens our shoulders to bear the weight of stress.

Architects and designers study how to distribute and transfer weight for stability and support. They do not confine the weight distribution to one beam. They know that one beam quickly becomes unsteady and warps. The same concept can get applied to relation-ships.

In a healthy relationship, the people involved share the decisions and combine the support. Their unique connection establishes an I-beam of partnered sup-port. However, in the abuser/abusee relationships, this connection gets lost. When each person in the re-lationship ends up singly coping and supporting daily stressors, the shape of the relationship will eventually warp.

As an individual, we confine ourselves by the boundaries that we design. And the model that we saw in chapter three illustrated the limitations that abusers create. Everyone can expand their space boundaries. They do not need tight restrictions. When people learn to communicate openly and honestly, they broaden their boundaries. In this manner, we each establish the type of support we need and where to receive it. And when our supports need reinforcing, each of us determines what kind of reinforcement will work for us. We should never concede our privilege of personal space to someone else's design, or we can end up as a doormat.

Some people may feel that they are too intelligent to get caught off guard and fall prey. However, they only delude themselves if they think they are exempt from a gaslighter's charms. Every individual opens their heart to someone or something every day. Gaslighters observe details to learn the secret to entering. And when they do join, we need to tell them to stop, leave, and go away. We will only end up hurting ourselves if we try to live with the abuse.

This book provided a lot of information to help people identify gaslighting abuse, escape away from it, and rebuild their lives. The time will come when we need to decide to put survival first. Survival first does not represent greed or selfishness; it means our appraisal of self-worth. A tiny seed of self-worth can develop into hope. Please use the information from these pages to improve your circumstances and help loved ones.

A survivor's love and hope for peaceful coexistence inspired the writing of this book. Only a survivor that traversed the road through abuse and recovery to a new life can identify with individuals that need help. We can offer them our experiences and hope. Inspire them with the evidence of our new and productive lives. And share our strength to discard the past, survive another day, and live until tomorrow.

Chapter 10

APPENDIX

APPENDIX

The feelings and emotions that people experience stem from reactions from personal esteem. These reactions can affect an individual's esteem positively, negatively, or straddle and waver. So, the organization of the lists reflects the effect on a person's esteem.

People in abusive environments learn to restrict their feelings to three possibilities – happy, numb, or sullen. Generally, people get so glad when they distance themselves from the abuser. We become numb when we hear the same comments and excuses repeatedly. And we become sullen when we suppress our anger. However, as we can see from the lists below, more than three feelings exist for everyone.

Typically, at first, we can identify the effect the feeling gives us. But as we heal emotionally away from the abuse, we experience a range of different emotions. Often, they rush at us, and we can only identify the effect.

POSITIVE: A - Adamant Affectionate B - Beautiful Blissful Bold Brave C - Calm Capable Caring Certain Cheerful Clever Contented D – Daring Decisive Delighted Determined E - Eager Ecstatic Empathetic Energetic Enthusiastic Excited Exhilarated F - Fascinated Flattered Free Full G - Gaiety Glad Glamorous Good Gratified H - Happy Helpful Honored Hopeful I – Immortal Impressed Infatuated Inspired J - Joyous K - Kind L - Lifted Loving M – Magnanimous N – Needed Nice Nutty P - Peaceful Pleased Pretty Proud R – Refreshed Relaxed Reverent Rewarded S - Satiated Satisfied Settled Sexy Silly Supported Sure Sympathetic T - Talkative Thankful U - Useful V - Vivacious W - Wonderful

INDIFFERENT: A – Adequate Ambivalent Anxious Apathetic Astounded B - Bored C - Childish Competitive Concerned Confused Conspicuous Consumed Contented Contrite Crazy D – Deceived Delayed Different Diminished Disappointed Discontented Discouraged Disposed of Distracted Distraught Disturbed Divided Doubtful Dubious E - Embarrassed Empty Exhausted F - Fearless Flustered Foolish Frantic G – Gullible H - Hassled Helpless Hesitant High Homesick Hysterical I - Ignored Imposed J - Jumpy M - Maudlin Miserable N – Naive Nervous O - Odd Old Overwhelmed P - Pensive Q – Quiet R –Relieved Resistant

Restless Resolute Righteous Rueful S - Scattered Shaky Shocked Skeptical Solemn Somber Startled Strange T - Tempted Tense Tentative Tired U - Uneasy Unhappy Unsettled V - Vehement Vulnerable W - Wiped Worried

NEGATIVE: A – Abandoned Angry Annoyed B - Bad Betrayed Bitter Burdened C - Challenged Cheated Cruel Crushed D – Deceitful Depressed Despair Desperate Despised Destructive Dominated Down Dubious Dumb Dumped E - Enraged Envious Evil F - Fearful Free Frightened Frustrated Furious G - Greedy Grief Guilty H - Hateful Hopeless Horrible Hurt I - Ignominious Insolent Intimidated Isolated J - Jealous K - Kicked L - Lame Lazy Lonely Loser Lost Low Lustful M - Mad Mean Morbid N – Nasty Naughty O - Obsessed Opposed Outraged P - Pained Panicked Persecuted Petrified Pressured Q - Quarrelsome Quiet R –Regretful Rejected Remorseful Ruined S - Sad Shame Small Sneaky Sorrowful Sorry Spiteful Stingy Strapped Stuck Stuffed Stupid Strained T - Tempestuous Terrible Terrified Threatened Trapped Troubled U - Ugly Used V - Violated Violent W - Wicked Woe Worthless

Once we begin getting comfortable identifying the range of different emotions, we can then start testing them. You can draw how the face looks for each feeling and emotion. Or stand at the mirror and watch as you try on each of the proper expressions for a sense. Matching a feeling to a facial expression sounds ridiculous but identifying feelings and emotions helps with recovery.

Frequently, people find that owning their feelings and emotions provides a sense of security and confidence. This confidence encourages the victim to further their recovery by acknowledging their vulnerabilities and weaknesses. Once a person can look at these personal aspects, they will gradually feel whole and worthwhile. Then you can grow through recovery and heal the heartbroken by gaslit disappointment and swallowed rage. Now you can find yourself and live the life that calls your name.

CPSIA information can be obtained
at www.ICGtesting.com
Printed in the USA
LVHW080054121122
732937LV00004B/683